...hold also the
ships, which
though they be so
great, and are
driven of fierce
winds, yet are
they turned about
with a very
Small Helm.

Small Helm Press interprets direction in contemporary life

Pearl Evans

HIDDEN DANGER
IN THE CLASSROOM

disclosure based
on ideas of W. R. Coulson

Small Helm Press

Petaluma, California

Library of Congress Cataloging- in-Publication Data

Evans, Pearl, 1927—
     Hidden danger in the classroom : disclosure based on ideas
of W. R. Coulson / by Pearl Evans
    p.   cm.
    Includes bibliographical references.
    ISBN 0-938453-04-1 (alk. paper) : $8.00
     1. Coulson, William R.--Views on education.
  2. Education--United States--Philosophy. 3. Education--United
States--Aims and objectives. 4. Education--United
States--Parent participation. I. Title.
LB885.C652E85   1990
370.11'0973--dc20   90-33415
                                  CIP

Copyright © 1990 by Pearl Evans

Design by Small Helm Press
This book may be ordered by mail from the publisher.
Please include $1.50 for shipping.
Small Helm Press
622-A Baker Street
Petaluma, California 94952

Manufactured in the United States of America
ISBN 0-938453-04-1

Library of Congress Catalog Card Number:
8 7 6 5 4 3 2 1

CONTENTS

ABOUT THE AUTHOR

Since her return from China in 1985, Pearl Evans has been writing full time. In recent years she has taken an active part concerning the educational issues of this book.

The author taught in public schools for over ten years and taught adults for seven years: English as a Foreign Language in the People's Republic of China one year, English as a Second Language to Indochinese one year, and adult education Bible Literature for five years. In her experience she has written public school curricula for two grades.

A graduate of the University of Texas, Austin, over the years she has since done extensive graduate work in education. For further background see the preface.

ABOUT WILLIAM R. COULSON
upon whose ideas this study is based

Holding two doctorates, one from the University of Notre Dame and one from the University of California at Berkeley, Dr. William R. Coulson is a licensed psychologist in California. He interned with the Psychotherapy Research Group of the Wisconsin Psychiatric Institute and the Neuropsychiatric Service of U.S. Veterans Administration Hospital in Phoenix.

Presently he is a guest lecturer at the University of San Diego. Also, he lectures nationwide on the dangers of affective, decision-making education, a movement he helped initiate with Carl Rogers and Abraham Maslow. Also, he is an active member of a group he helped create, the Center for Enterprising Families, a nonprofit, tax exempt scientific corporation, home of the Research Council on Ethnopsychology since 1977.

During the previous presidential administration, Coulson was consultant to Georgetown University Medical School in Washington, D.C. and was a member of the Technical Advisory Panel on Drug Education Curricula for the United States Department of Education.

Coulson was research associate to Rogers and Maslow at the Western Behavioral Sciences Institute in La Jolla, California. There he directed a program in the philosophy of science, led the post-doctoral research training program, and helped Rogers organize the country's first program of facilitator training. Later, he helped Rogers found the Center for Studies of the Person. Also Coulson and Rogers edited for Charles E. Merrill, a major textbook firm, a series of seventeen volumes on humanistic education. And for his expertise in this field, Coulson has been called to testify in court.

PREFACE and acknowledgment

"What is your philosophy of life?" I heard my father ask again and again of friends and acquaintances. Along with an interest in that question, I've acquired a fascination for the intricacies of human relatedness. Therefore, since before I became a parent or longtime schoolteacher, I have valued the concerns of psychology. (My son John is a clinical psychologist in San Diego.) Nevertheless, I do take exception to the psychotherapeutic approach in the classroom.

In recent years, when I discovered harmful influences at work in education, I became concerned but felt overwhelmed by the strength of entrenched power. But not until mid 1989, when I read an article by psychologist William R. Coulson, did I see a spark of hope for America's schools. My confidence rests in knowing that Coulson's record of firsthand experience and compilation of research facts furnish solid evidence that confirms what I know.

As former colleague of both Carl Rogers and Abraham Maslow, whose ideas carried psychotherapy into the classroom, Coulson holds a unique position. He knows the harm done by this educational movement. At first an enthusiastic supporter of this humanistic approach, later a reluctant one, and finally, one who could see clearly, Coulson warns about the harm that data analysis shows about behavior that results from this education.

While producing this book, I read other books by or about Coulson, Maslow, Rogers, and the movement to get a broader picture against which to verify and from which to amplify what I say. Another safeguard for reliability has been my contact with Coulson. And, of course, my own background keeps me on target—as an educator in the classroom, in graduate education classes, in writing curriculum; also my part as a citizen in monitoring the curriculum and activity of local schools.

From Coulson's papers, conversation, audio and video tapes, I chose those ideas that correspond to the topics of this book. Then with wide reading, observation, and experience, by assimilation I distilled points or principles for each chapter.

Since the ideas of William R. Coulson agree with my own in all essential elements of the subject, I acknowledge to the reader that most of what I present are his ideas, sometimes even his phraseology. Consequently, his ideas and my comments so intertwine that I cannot credit him continually without breaking continuity; I do credit him on significant portions, however.

I am grateful for access to the numerous published Coulson articles and papers, which writings are listed in the bibliography. With Dr. Coulson's consent I present this book, much of which is a reorganized paraphrase of his writing and speaking.

May this study contribute to making the classroom a safe and sane place for learning.

Pearl Evans

1 WHAT IS THIS EDUCATION THAT HARMS?

BEGINNINGS AND BACKGROUND

In 1960 Bill Coulson discovered Carl Rogers.

"I remember I was sitting in the kitchen in our barracks apartment at the University of California, Berkeley," he writes. "I was studying counseling. On that day reading *Client-Centered Therapy* by Rogers I turned to my wife and said, 'This man knows what I know—but he's been able to say it. . . Too bad he's dead.' 'What makes you think he's dead?' Jeannie asked. 'Because that's the sort of luck I have.'" So taken was Coulson with this man and his teaching that to have a chance to meet him lay outside his comprehension.

He did meet Rogers, but not until he moved with his family to Wisconsin for study and research. Then he had a chance to tell his favorite psychologist how much his book meant to him. "I'm really excited to meet you," Coulson told him. Rogers looked, paused, and said, "I can see that." With that first handshake, Coulson experienced the intense, empathic "client-centered approach" of Carl Rogers.

In Wisconsin, after meeting Rogers, Coulson's excitement did not wane. When soon Rogers moved to California, Coulson packed up his family and followed. There he teamed up with Rogers at the Western Behavioral Sciences Institute and later with him founded the Center for Studies of the Person in La Jolla.[1]

After success with client-centered therapy in the clinic, Rogers developed an approach for the general population. From this sprang the sixties human potential movement, which transformed society's values and eventually the thinking of educators. About the changed thinking of the sixties, Daniel Yankelovich, national social researcher, writes, "The New Values represent the breakdown of previous moral norms and are characterized by the rejection of authority, emphasis on the emotional rather than the rational, freer sexual morality, strong accent on self and self-fulfillment, acceptability of illegal drugs, and a more informal life style."[2]

During that time, when Rogers applied his person-centered approach to education, enthusiasm ran high, because everyone expected the experiments to yield good dividends. But they didn't. Results showed that this education harms children. Nevertheless, Carl Rogers and Abraham Maslow popularized humanistic psychology nationwide; as their young colleague, Coulson did his part to spread their ideas.

Coulson regrets his part in helping Rogers introduce this psychotherapeutic way of life into the schools. Let me add that although he opposes psychotherapy in the classroom, he is not anti-psychology, for he practices and teaches psychology and at times witnesses miracles of healing.[3] What he opposes is inappropriate application of therapy to settings outside the clinic. For what works within the profession does not necessarily work universally elsewhere for others.

Abraham Maslow also had second thoughts. Before he died in 1970, he retracted his support for this educational movement. The withdrawal of Coulson was more gradual although his questions and doubts began early, too. Later Carl Rogers also acknowledged that his team's experimentation produced "a pattern of failure," even though he did not blame the method. Yet in spite of all evidence, in the 1990s educational policy makers continue to support this education that harms children.

GENERIC FEATURES

With variations on a common theme, education that harms crops up at different times and places. Only the name changes. Titles proliferate because once the public catches on to the nature of a program in one place, the same curriculum re-emerges somewhere else under a new title. And with each new generic name comes a description of some other feature of the programs. For example, the *person-centered approach* is the name Carl Rogers chose to indicate that the base of this education is similar to his client-centered therapy.

The name *humanistic education* describes the program philosophy. Under this banner, education stakes out new territory beyond the experiential humanism of pioneer educator John Dewey. It no longer focuses on real-world subject matter, the legitimate domain of education, but on the inner life, heretofore the exclusive domain of the family, the church, and private life. Thus, administrators make new claims of authority over the psyches of children because they claim traditional education and family teachings are inadequate for "times of rapid change." Old ways cannot meet new demands, they say.

This mindset perceives as disadvantaged every child taught religion by his parents. For this reason humanistic educators rally their forces to counteract such molding of children "into conforming robots."[4] To the extent of the effectiveness of parental teaching—to that extent—modern theory declares the integrity of a child's own choices compromised, Coulson states.

Humanistic education rejects other molds of objective standards, too, not just family-gendered ones. Thus, this model robs the young of high aspirations and sends them out ill equipped to face the world.

The *New Age* movement concurs with these ideas. "To be free, says Marilyn Ferguson, author of *Age of Aquarius,* children have to be free from us. "At times this means teaching for healthy, appropriate rebellion, not conformity. Maturity brings with it a morality that derives from the innermost self, not from mere obedience to the culture's mores."[5]

A popular label for this teaching is *decision making education.* Some home economics texts that Coulson examined urge that the process be applied widely, from small things like "buying a new pair of shoes. . . to more complex decisions such as those which involve religious preferences; education and career choices; the use of alcohol, tobacco, and drugs; and sexual habits." In these programs the teacher gives selected information or hypothetical situations and asks, "What would you do?"[6]

A logical label for this education is *psychotherapeutic education,* but because that name calls attention to inadequate training for teachers, it is seldom used. Often training is an expensive three-day workshop for a select group of teachers, who then teach the rest of the faculty.

Values clarification is another self-describing name. This label has fallen into disrepute because it allows outsiders to see that this education challenges parental and societal values. Its hypothesis is that one person cannot know what is good for another. From this, the child learns to look on what adults teach—including what parents uphold—not as truth to live by, but as one of many options. Other names are *values education* and *value-free education.*

A more popular title, *nondirective education,* describes the hands-off policy of the presiding teacher. The teacher as facilitator sets up the group situation and enforces the rules of the game. Without interfering, the adult leader lets the child explore alternatives with his peers.

Within this framework, nondirective education is supposed to be *value-free education.* But if you examine the program closely, you see that the decision making process applies *only* to selected topics. For topics like sex, drugs, suicide the student decides for himself. But in matters important to program creators, the student is not allowed to make up his own mind. At that point nondirective programs become directive; for example, programs *prescribe* attitudes and vocabulary concerning homosexuality. Value-free education, in fact, is not neutral; it promotes an agenda.

Process education places importance on process itself, not on content. It endorses a way of life. The multi-step process bases decision making and values choosing not on morality but according to feelings, alternatives and consequences.

Affective or *experiential education* is feeling-centered as opposed to rational or cognitive. Affective education teaches the child to be in touch with all of his feelings, especially negative ones, such as anger, hate, fear, grief, confusion. For only by uncensored expression of these can the child grow and develop fully, and only in this way can he establish his own identity, theorists say.

Self-esteem building describes another generic feature of this education. Instead of encouraging children to earn self esteem through achievement in scholastic and extracurricular activities, this education exalts self-worth as an end in itself. The self emphasis makes the child his own authority, the center of his universe, his own god. "You are the most important person in your life," says the text of *Today's Teen*. "You are the designer of your life. . .*You are not a 'chip off the old block,'*" says another text (emphasis added).[7]

Teachers accept student self-expression unconditionally, and they tell students they are fine just as they are. Eager to disallow the possibility of a child's failure, the psychologized teacher must also disallow the possibility of success; nothing need be striven for, nothing brought under control, for nothing is amiss. Dispensing self-esteem is this education's magic answer for healing social ills.[8]

GROUP WORK

Class time in nondirective education revolves around group activities, with peer-group discussion the most important. As facilitator, the teacher withholds direction and "accepts whatever vision of the world students proclaim."[9] In theory, any opinion is valid. In practice, though, any opinion is acceptable except one expressing belief in morality or truth, especially if stated with conviction—because that's being "judgmental" and can disqualify a student from participation. And any opinion is acceptable unless it agrees with a student's family values; then the student is open to challenge and to the possibility of humiliation. Decision making education has for its frame of reference only feelings, alternatives and consequences. By excluding morality from consideration on topics that by their nature require moral choice, the programs teach relativism and deny absolutes, except for one—the absolute that there are no absolutes. By making parental values one of many choices, this approach threatens to undermine whatever truth the child learns at home. It subjectivizes morality.

Besides emphasizing the subjective over the objective, affective education emphasizes group work over individual achievement; cooperative learning over competitive work; collective activity over individual leadership; facilitation over teaching; trust over accountability.

Group work activities vary but are subjective in content: soul-baring discussions, peer input and peer counseling, games, interviews and questionnaires, simulations (recreating real life situations), exercises based on sociograms—including group criticism of a child, composition, journals, psycho-drama, socio-drama, role playing, puppetry, guided imagery meditations and relaxation techniques,[10] selected films, art, poetry, and music activities, contests—sometimes sponsored by New Age groups[11]—and intercultural projects and trips.

Intercultural activities in elementary school often center on those of folktale origin, which include simulated religious experiences. Favorite folktale sources are Native American and Nordic or Celtic, whose religions have spiritist and animist origins.[12]

Relaxation activities may incorporate elements of Eastern mysticism or primitive earth-religion ideas.[13] Guided meditation can be a means of "controlled daydreaming," in which the participant remains active and aware of everything but nonetheless undergoes a form of hypnosis.

Group activities, such as conflict resolution and communication skills, emphasize the democratic relationships between child and teacher. These skills recommend I-messages in place of you-messages. Instead of the teacher saying, "*You* are rude" and eliciting the thought, "He thinks I am bad," the teacher says, "*I'm* frustrated when you say that." Then the door remains open to work on the problem of relating to each other. The teacher respects the pupil and actively listens to what he has to say. This technique, of course, has its good points and is often appropriate.[14]

In the philosophy's full implementation, however, this leveling technique eliminates authority status, and the formula response discourages individuality. "The only difference between you and your child,"

says Thomas Gordon, protege of Rogers and proponent of conflict resolution, "is that one of you is older."[15] This egalitarianism, a mark of education that harms, fails to note that adults have experience and knowledge children lack and need.

Yet authority challenged is not the most volatile element of nondirective group activity. Risk-taking as a way of life invites experimentation
in dangerous activity. "By risk-taking," a text for educators says, "we
mean the chance one often takes when one ventures out of one's pattern
of behavior. . . It is safe to say that regardless of the risk involved, the
greatest risk would come from not exercising the opportunity to risk—
and possibly to grow from it."[16]

A West Coast school fundraising letter puts the idea this way:

> Come to the edge, He said
> They said, We are afraid,
> Come to the edge, He said
> They did.
> He pushed them and they flew.

Risk-taking can be a healthy part of growth and adventuresomeness. But
playing Russian roulette is something else. The good child, who trusts his
teacher, considers the alternatives of doing drugs and makes his decision.
But the risk is too great.

"[Now] we're picking up the people who are falling off the cliff as
they get more and more years into their habit," says an administrator of
the U.S. Alcohol, Drug Abuse, and Mental Health Administration.[17]

Next, let's look at training for group work in specific, packaged
programs. Two of them, known by brand names Quest and Here's
Looking at You (HLAY), typify the gross medical amateurism of teacher
training. In an expensive, sixteen to twenty hour workshop, teachers
learn to play group games they will later teach the children to play.

About the group work, here's what a Project Charlie coordinator said:
"It's fun time. It's not—we don't sit there and lecture at all. We have
activities and we have just neat little things that we do and just all kinds
of—I mean, they don't sit in their seats. We get them out of their seats
and we do, you know, sit on the floor and just have a really good time."

This speech reflects the lack of professionalism that dominates group
work. Coulson quotes it here in order to suggest that affective education
is not only nonacademic but *anti*academic in carelessness of speech and
in enthusiasm for sitting on the floor. He does not attack good-hearted
individuals. In observing these programs in his travels, almost everyone

he met was good-hearted. But with the life and death issues of decision making education, good-heartedness is not enough, he says.

An example of an activity Coulson challenges is one that follows no standards or norms for behavior. It's called Break-in from the Quest program. "You get to tickle, push, and touch your classmates," the program says. Then afterwards students discuss their feelings.[18]

Topics for discussion in the DECIDE drug program, are questionable, too. Students discuss whether or not to lie, steal, cheat, or vandalize, and whether or not to tell on friends who do these things.

A mother told Coulson that her neighbor observed a sixth grade session of this program. The topic was stealing versus loyalty. And what was the nondirected group consensus? Don't tell on the thief, and negotiate for half the take. With no intervention from the nondirective facilitator team, that ended the matter. The neighbor himself sat with lips sealed because he had entered the class on condition that he remain aloof. Since the children had mastered "active listening," "I-messages," and other communication skills, nothing remained for the teacher or observer to do, except perhaps to hurry home and lock the doors.

The mother in question, however, had no such choice. She had to live with this new way of life. For her son had learned at age eleven that personal integrity depends on two things: first, you do only what you decide freely, and second, you make your choice from a list of alternatives. Since his mother offered no alternatives, the son drew up his own list. Not surprisingly, he rated all alternatives higher than doing household chores. "I will no longer perform these jobs," he announced.[19]

TOPICS

Whatever the topics chosen to fulfill the goals of these programs, group activities remain almost the same. And behind everything lies the same philosophy that defines the person of tomorrow. This future person sees religious institutions as irrelevant, if not damaging; has little regard for marriage; welcomes transient relationships; endorses "turning on" with drugs; is feeling-centered, always changing; and sets no restraints or limits to human possibilities. This is what Rogers told 1969 graduates at Sonoma State University.[20]

Translated into educational goals, this philosophy proposes to teach a way of life, to free up behavior, and to change the way children look at the world.

These goals find fulfillment in the teaching of the following specific topics: death and dying, depression, suicide; stress management, relaxation techniques, coping skills; body, disease prevention, AIDS; homemaking, family life, sex, abortion, sexual abuse, "alternate life-styles"; addiction, drug education; personal identity or self-image, independence, communication skills, conflict resolution, interpersonal relationships, peer counseling; globalism, environmentalism; nonjudgmentalism, egalitarianism, children's rights. And the same goals find fulfillment in many special services such as mentor programs, gifted and talented programs, and classroom guidance counseling sessions.

High on the list of topics taught by the decision making model are drug and sex education. Since risk-taking, life without moral restraint, and "turning on" are hallmarks of this philosophy, experimentation with sex and drugs offer a vehicle for playing out movement objectives. Although education cannot with the public's blessing endorse experimentation for minor children, it can present sexual activity and drug use in the framework of decision making. And it can place the choice outside the realm of morality.

In line with the aim of the sixties movement to break down previous moral norms, affective sex education gives equal status to all lifestyles: None are deviant or immoral, only different but acceptable. Therefore, sex education is not for the purpose of physiological information as in a traditional health class but to give the topic a new spin, a psychologized, humanistic viewpoint.

"In many urban centers, AIDS education includes, and at times seems dominated by, a homosexual perspective," Coulson writes. "The emphasis is on the inevitability—indeed the rightness—of yielding to sexual urges." In the spring of 1987, Coulson sampled a week of AIDS education at a San Diego County high school and witnessed promotion of the New Values.

The speaker from the San Diego AIDS Project was a man, whose foremost qualification for teaching was that he had AIDS. He showed a film, which lacked all perspective on abstinence and which New York parents had rejected.

After giving graphic details about sex habits of gay men, the speaker answered a question about how he got AIDS. "I don't know," he said. "I tried to think back to the late seventies. I had a lover for three years when I was your age. I was doing drugs and I was having a lot of sex. I don't know how I got it. *I was a typical teenager.*"

He concluded his talk by romanticizing even the disease itself, by saying he'd met some wonderful, inspiring, beautiful people he never would have met. Having AIDS, he said, "is an incredible, incredible journey."[21] Afterwards, in honor of the AIDS-dignitary, a group of student council members crowded around to have their photo taken with him.

When promoting the movement, Coulson said that he did not realize his team's part in encouraging homosexuality. Looking back, he sees that whether approaching the subject in the name of risk-taking, personal courage, intimacy, or the claims of the present, they nonetheless conditioned people to be homosexual.[22]

From today's perspective, Coulson sees that to teach sexual abstinence as the standard for minor children is not heavy handed. Rather, to give direction is to give children freedom. And to withhold direction is to underestimate the ability of the young to respond positively to the good advice of those who care about them, he says.

Let me give an example by contrasting the effects of school policies. Some school officials used to designate areas of high school campuses for smoking. Students will smoke no matter what you do, administrators and boards rationalized at the time. But now with more evidence of the dangers and addictiveness of tobacco use, public opinion will no longer tolerate smoking on campus. So, designated smoking areas have disappeared, and smoking by young people has dropped dramatically. With the help of adult constraint, students in their formative years do learn to live by better standards.

Yet regarding sex, educators continue to rope off areas of children's lives for so-called safe sex with condoms "because they're going to do it anyway." The public still allows this implied consent, if not promotion, for teenage sex. And sexual activity increases at ever earlier ages.

Just as modern sex education fits the sixties norm, today's drug education also retains a sixties flavor. In that earlier decade, "turning on" with drugs was a new way to experience life; it was a means to expand consciousness. Sixties people used to talk about recreational drugs and responsible drug use in the same way people talk about safe sex today.[23]

Although public opinion grows stronger daily against drug use, program writers for drug education today continue to express lack of conviction about whether drug use is harmful. What they communicate to the student is that if he decides to make a buy, his decision is beyond criticism—so long as the decision is his own.

Because a person-centered approach demands risk-taking for the sake of growth, it presents drug use as a matter about which children choose.

Yes, it's true that programs tell children they *can* say no—*it's all right to say no*—but they still present alternative, dangerous behavior as a viable option. "We don't stress the negative," a police officer/teacher from the DARE program explained to me.

Coulson says that in decision making education for the nonusing child, no longer are drugs something foreign to his personal life; under school influence, drugs move from periphery to center stage, demanding attention. The decision itself becomes paramount, a chance to express independence. With curiosity piqued, the pupil explores, experiments, "grows." What before seemed evil, he now feels "liberated" to choose.[24]

In the decision making process, the nonusing student interacts with peers from whom he might otherwise feel obliged to distance himself. His resistance to drugs breaks down in the group because the line of influence flows from the user to the nonuser, research surveyor Daniel Yankelovich reports.[25]

With recent pressure from public opinion, schools now add "refusal skills" to the process. But what if the child *decides* not to refuse drugs but to accept them? The decision making model claims its strength to be that the child makes his own choices. Therefore, a student will think, "Adults say they want us to make our own decisions about drugs, but really they want us to say no." Children are not dumb: If the criterion of a successful program is to withhold direction, then a child concludes that whatever he chooses forwards the program.[26] But if in a decision making program, he's not allowed to make the decision, aren't the signals mixed?

Besides, Coulson agrees that no matter how many improvements are made within the nondirective, value-free framework, so long as the peer-group, decision making program is taught in the prescribed way and remains in place, this is education that harms children.

2 THE FAILED TEST OF EXPERIENCE

ABRAHAM MASLOW REJECTED THIS EDUCATION

Coulson believes Daddy Abraham Maslow[1] would join him and the men of Nevermore in asking, "By what right does the state—in the name of family life education—impose a particular morality that leads to dangerous behavior? By what right does the state claim spiritual authority over the souls of school children, or for that matter psychological authority over their psyches?"

Nevermore is a small group of family men who once worked with Carl Rogers and other leaders of humanistic psychology. They claim the late Abraham Maslow as a member of Nevermore because he set an example for them in his renunciation of affective, decision making education for children.[2]

Coulson likes to call this man Daddy Maslow because he was big enough to admit when he was wrong. Maslow once believed "that the world will either be saved by psychologists. . . or else it will not be saved at all." "We have to teach everyone to be a therapist,"[3] he told a *Life* reporter. Later, he admitted that was a big mistake. He also admitted he had been wrong to endorse cultural relativism.[4]

And Coulson calls this man Daddy Maslow because Maslow had a moral and scholastic heritage that he wanted to pass along to future generations. Although liberal in his thinking, in morality—as a Jewish father and grandfather—he drew a line beyond which he would not go. And as a professor in a Jewish university, he passed along to others his high regard for learning. His moral heritage saved him from radical behavior, and his academic heritage, in the end, saved him from overextension of his ideas; he *would not* abandon this legacy.

In 1958 on the eve of the sixties movement, Maslow said that a society without a value system breeds psychological disorder because children need to be directed. Setting limits and employing consistent discipline are essential for children, he said.[5]

So you see his philosophy never was self-indulgent, touchy-feely, or a do-your-own-thing principle. Others carried his idea in that direction. Maslow always upheld academic authority and scholarship. And because decision making programs in public schools undermine authority and impede scholarship, he opposed them—even though he did not at first express his discontent except in private writings.

Maslow was the one who laid the groundwork to make humanistic psychology acceptable in the wider scholastic community. And from his pioneering, a likeminded professional network sprang up through which Carl Rogers and many others kept in touch. In 1961 during a year's sabbatical, Maslow became a resident participant with Carl Rogers, Coulson, and others at Western Behavioral Sciences Institute. By that time this renowned psychologist had distinguished himself in many ways: He wrote for the initial volume of the *Journal of Humanistic Psychology*, was former president of the American Psychological Association, and was a distinguished professor at Brandeis University.

Maslow had gained a reputation because he lifted psychology to a higher level: from concentration on methodology to philosophical considerations; also from the pathology of the abnormal to the study of outstanding human beings. In his famous pyramid of needs, he did not stop with the animal-like needs of human beings; "self-actualization," or self-fulfillment, he placed at the peak of human development. These new views became extraordinarily popular.[6]

What began in the sixties as pop psychology has become in the nineties holy writ. Today these ideas are authoritative for writing whole, new curricula, kindergarten through twelfth grade. Such *affective* programs include topics that used to be approached academically in courses on communications, family living, home economics, and health education. Unfortunately, the outcome has been national moral decline and academic loss. And because of his cultural heritage, this upset Maslow.

Also, moral irresponsibility in the human potential movement bothered him. In his journal he called the more radical followers "jungle people" and said they would have to be fought off as such, giving no quarter. He repudiated anarchic behavior; he didn't want young followers to credit him with having invented something alien to his own way of life and thinking.[7]

As the movement progressed, his rancor increased. Before his death, Maslow in his journal denounced those groups for which once he held high hopes: not only Esalen Institute at Big Sur, the foremost humanistic psychology outpost, but also hippie culture, psychology 3, Synanon, and

National Training Laboratories (NTL) for training business and government leaders. Maslow finished his journal diatribe by saying he opposed the whole Eupsychian network—his name for hundreds of groups interested in humanistic psychology. In the end he saw the movement as a revival of old philosophies and issues: romanticism, anti-intellectualism, and abusiveness of scientific principles.[8]

In 1965 because nondirective, value-free education had created a moral vacuum, Maslow lectured at Brandeis about *The Taboo of Tenderness: The Disease of Valuelessness:* "Innocence can be redefined and called stupidity. Honesty can be called gullibility. Candor becomes lack of common sense. Interest in your work can be called cowardice. Generosity can be called softheadedness, and observe: The former word is disturbing, the latter is not. It can be dealt with. You can deal with a jerk or a fool or a pollyanna or something of the sort. [But] nobody knows how to deal with an honest man."[9]

Besides helping him see moral deficiency in the movement, Maslow's cultural heritage made him aware of academic failure, too. His ethnic antennae, constantly up at Brandeis, told him that something was wrong in the classroom. His observations forced him to be honest: His students had become centers of decision making universes, all their own. No one could tell them about right and wrong or anything else. Therefore, he feared students might lose their best chance to develop good minds capable of continuing a long and hallowed tradition of scholarship and professional attainment. He wanted Brandeis students to enter into this disciplined inheritance and would have rejected vehemently any psychologist's intimation that such a wish was selfish.[10]

Maslow's journal entry in April 1966 contradicts the philosophy of nondirective, peer-group work in the classroom: The essence of teaching is not for the adult to listen but *to author,* "to speak while others listen, or to publish for others to study, that is, to lecture," he wrote. The dialogue part of teaching he restricted to efforts to ascertain if the listener truly understands the speaker. Maslow had received from his forebears and he had something he wanted to pass along.[11]

"My class has lost the traditional Jewish respect for knowledge, learning, and teachers," Maslow wrote about his last university class in January 1969. "This rebellion is *not* just a generation gap. It's the first time in history that students have repudiated their teachers, which means loss of all tacit knowledge, apprentice training, demonstration by the master, showing how—which means a generation of lousy professionals." Maslow wrote that you can't learn medicine or plumbing or chemistry through encounter groups, in discussion circles, or by looking within yourself.[12]

He mourned the loss of a long standing educational ideal. And he knew that in some ways his romantic writing about self-fulfillment was to blame. Students in quest of self learned to reject authority outside themselves—including the authority of an increasingly concerned Professor Abraham Maslow himself. His classroom position of authority had fallen by the hand of his own students. For they wanted discussion and interpersonal encounter. They wanted "process." They inclined to hearing themselves talk; Maslow inclined to having them listen.[13] "I have tended to see this as one symptom of the extreme child-centering of recent decades," Maslow wrote in his journal. "That is, all adults present are supposed to stop talking and listen to the child. He may interrupt the adults, but the adults dare not interrupt him."[14]

As he could now see, classrooms full of youthful selves were turning out to be classrooms full of youthful unteachables. In one class, to which he gave an assignment, a young woman said to him, "I will read these books if I want to and if I don't want to, I won't."[15] After that class, Maslow eliminated from his book on personality any passages that might imply that children could be the proper subjects to which to apply his concept of self-actualization.

In spite of the fact that his own earlier writings on self-actualization were partly to blame for this outcome, Maslow chose to heed the danger signals. His heritage along with his scientific instincts combined to make him willing to risk his reputation in denouncing a movement to which he gave the first impetus.[16]

For the most part, however, Maslow wrote only privately about his displeasure; it took time for his resolve to strengthen. At first he called the decision making programs soft and goody-goody. But as time went by, he became stronger in his criticism. By the end of his life, he was writing copy that he saw as "blunter, more honest, more naked, more true and correct." And yet, when he projected his life ahead to the age of seventy, he predicted that he'd probably look back and decide his current writings were not naked enough and too timid. If only he could thunder like the patriarchal, biblical prophets! Maslow fantasized in his journal.[17] Had he reached the age of seventy—he died at sixty-two—he might have done just that, even if he did claim to be an atheist.

Maslow's renunciation of the therapeutic classroom remains virtually unknown to this day. He had a series of heart attacks that prevented his making a comprehensive revision of his theories before he died. And the later retractions that are available remain unread and unheeded. The only Maslow now acknowledged is the earlier, romantic Maslow. And so the public does not know the truth about this great man's assessment of the educational movement. And students continue to pay the lifelong price of moral confusion and forfeited academic instruction.

In their last months together, early every morning the elder Maslows had long talks about the state of the world, including the havoc caused by too little respect for intellect. They agreed that Maslow's earlier attempts at retraction had misled people because his words were too "hedged, fudged, appeasing, diplomatic, polite."[18]

Maslow planned to write a more comprehensive retraction of the therapeutic lifestyle as an ideal way of life. The full correction got sketched in his journals but never readied for publication. Sometimes he called his plan of revision an "Esalen critique" or "a critique of self-actualization." About this report, Ed Hoffman said that Maslow in the spring of 1970 knew it would lose him many devotees, but he was so disenchanted by what had resulted, he had to be honest.[19] His widow Bertha wished he could have fulfilled his desire to write that critique. In 1988 she told Coulson and his wife, "I'm really very, very sorry he never got to do that. It was the next thing he was going to do; this self-actualization thing. It was so misunderstood and misused."

Before he died, Maslow had time for only one brief but pointed article of dissent, "Humanistic Education vs. Professional Education," which was not published until 1979, nine years after his death.[20] And he wrote a second, polished piece, which appeared as a preface for the posthumous edition of his seminal work, *Motivation and Personality*.[21] In it he asserted that "self-actualization" should "very definitely" never have been applied to children. Maslow saw the demand to "actualize" as something that could be used against the young by forces that coveted them for their increasing purchasing power.[22]

One record of Maslow's retraction is in *The Right to be Human* by Edward Hoffman. "[Maslow became] drained by some of the contradictions he saw in his own theory of self-actualization," Dr. Hoffman writes.[23] Another record of Maslow's disappointment is in *The Journals of A. H. Maslow*, published in 1979.

For the last eighteen months of his life, Maslow knew without a doubt that the therapeutic classroom never should have been tried; he deplored the harm done to children[24]. He believed the young deserve to be protected. Yet he saw children subjected to group programs that he claimed less than one percent of adults can survive without a very great fall.[25] From his vantage viewpoint as designer of humanistic psychology in the clinic, he could see what made this education fail in the classroom—not foot-dragging schoolboards or conservative parents but the faulty concept behind the programs. He wanted to halt the trend, but it was too late. His idea had taken on a life of its own.[26]

Even more shocking than witnessing the effect on his students, Abraham Maslow saw his own children harmed. Experiments in classroom group work were underway before the Maslow offspring were independent. He saw the development of a daughter compromised. The child had possessed potential. She had a calling, which her father identified as the family's "Jewish heritage of books and libraries." But in 1970 Maslow died believing his daughter lost that birthright.[27]

Maslow turned around before Coulson did. While he pondered retractions, Rogers and Coulson went on working on the textbook series they were co-editing. By the mid-seventies the self-theory attained the status of revealed truth. If anything, in 1990 it has since grown the more religious.[28]

"Maslow and I both entered this movement with fanfare and left the scene with hardly a word," says Coulson. And that's why Coulson now sets the record straight for both of them. He knows Daddy Maslow would like that.[29]

COULSON REJECTED THIS EDUCATION

Within the boundaries of structured therapy sessions, the ability of Rogers to convey unconditional acceptance to his clients had been good. His deep acceptance took clients further into their own responsibilities before God; it made them more truthful. It has been the export of his beliefs outside the clinic that causes harm in schools.

The first large scale attempt to export this approach to schools was conducted by the Center for the Studies of the Person (CSP), an institution Coulson helped found with Carl Rogers. The team of psychotherapists wanted to test the hypothesis that in a major school system, good things happen when administrators, faculty, and students interact in all areas of the system. Their aim was to inspire creative teaching, more student responsibility, with more democracy and better communication system-wide. The new creed was to encompass *all* of life, not just present experience, not just campus life. A disillusioned project leader later spoke of their vision as "the whole-world thing."

The approach they used in this school system was similar to present day decision making programs in that it shared a common philosophy and methodology. It was feeling-centered and group oriented; it did not, however, set up the specific topics of current educational projects.

In due time, CSP found for the project both a fund donor and a school system to volunteer to risk this offbeat undertaking. The donor was the R. J. Reynolds family through the Mary Reynolds Babcock Foundation. The school system belonged to the Order of the Immaculate Heart of Mary, six hundred sisters known for their innovative thinking. The system had a Los Angeles college, three high schools, and about fifty-six elementary schools on the West Coast.[30]

This person-centered approach at the college campus brought one change immediately: Academic study suffered because group therapy interfered. Teachers, after intensive encounter sessions, didn't want to teach and students didn't want to learn; they all wanted to "relate."[31]

But in the beginning, no one worried about that because everyone entered into the spirit of the project. Participants at Immaculate Heart College welcomed impromptu group discussion: They became acquainted on a deeper level, developed team spirit, and appreciated the respect due each person.[32] But as informal reports began to reveal deeper, ideological aims for the project, the faculty began to catch on: Something more *total* was expected of them; some sort of conversion should take place, they sensed. At this they balked. They didn't want to become therapeutic ideals divested of their living, breathing personhood.

Students, too, had misgivings. One said the psychologists were like invaders, an occupying force. But team members didn't see themselves that way; they came to liberate. And because of confidence in their ideals, they were able to ignore faculty protests—for the school's own good, of course. For although project leaders met complainants with empathic, active listening, they didn't miss a beat in fulfilling their schedule. Their therapy, successful in a limited setting, became oppressive when it leaped the bounds.[33]

Why did the theory break down? Faculty saw the problem this way: Whereas project psychologists spoke of truth only as *perceived* truth— not as objective truth—these same ones set themselves up to judge differing perceptions. Claiming to be anti-authority, project leaders became the ultimate authority. That's why the faculty said they had to fight. They clung to diversity of freely exchanged ideas and rejected the person-centered model.[34]

With reluctance, the team withdrew, and the college expired. Within three and a half years, 315 of the 600 nuns had petitioned to leave the order.[35] Today only a lay organization of Catholics and non-Catholics exists. And it has no official status within the church. Whatever change might have been accomplished, the institution and many private lives disintegrated. Though other reasons might be cited, one faculty member explained the bustup in the project's own terms: The project "facilitated the action."[36]

This was not the only school system the CSP team had to leave. In a chapter called "A Pattern of Failure," in *Freedom to Learn for the 80's,* Rogers documented other failures. They had to leave a series of schools, in no small part because host educators felt the psychologists disregarded their point of view.[37]

In the team's eyes, the person-centered approach defined a superior form of reality so total that when evidence began to show failure, the team from the Center for the Studies of the Person looked outside the theory for cause of failure. Breakdown resulted from faculty or administrative recalcitrance, some of them said. With each subsequent failure, this explanation became more official.

The psychologists were surprised at the outcome. It's hard to believe, but each failure for the team thereafter was a brand-new surprise. And that's still true. Administrators at Bainbridge Island in 1989 registered the same disbelief at the statistics showing failure of their twelve year program. It is as if believers learn nothing from experience—their own or others. Certainly their faith doesn't crumble; they continue to see traditional schools as bastions of oppression that need the therapeutic model to humanize them.[38]

Originally, the ideal of being less self-centered called Coulson to enter psychology in order to help people and to satisfy what he conceived to be a general human obligation. Later, having become more "psychologized," he was able to trace this sense of obligation to his early training. Therefore, after he learned to believe that he should author his own values, he felt the need to shake loose from early influences.

He didn't realize he was trading one influence for another. Nor did he see that "being good to himself" would fail to make him the "fully functioning person" he wanted to become. Nor did he want to admit that at some point the project team had stopped testing their hypothesis and had started selling it.

Finally, however, since he is an empiricist, Coulson reached a day of reckoning. He had to acknowledge that evidence negated what he and his colleagues claimed. In time, therefore, Coulson dropped out.

At last, now he is able to accept the possibility and reality of selflessness in others. He no longer has to read selfish motives into all the actions he witnesses. He no longer has to reject his parents' model simply because of their strong, early influence.[39]

In tracing Coulson's own wandering away from youthful intentions, I can see the footprints of society's journey astray as well. Like many today, he tried for a while to disregard the danger signals. He didn't like to believe the facts: Maybe something was wrong with the testing; maybe this, maybe that. But study after study confirms those original findings. As time goes by, more research and more experience convinces Coulson that these psychotherapeutic ideas in education are not merely wrong for minor children; they're pernicious. To ask children to look within for the answers is a terrible mistake; they need the direction of those under whose care they live, Coulson says.

Coulson regrets his part in establishing nondirective, decision making programs in the schools.

3 THE FAILED TEST OF RESEARCH

RESEARCH

It's fun, teachers and students agree. Workshop-trained facilitators give decision making education rave reviews.[1] But "self-esteem" talk notwithstanding, all major scientific data analysis on decision making education records the solemn truth: It puts children's lives at risk. Nevertheless, in the 1990s such programs continue to take off in our schools.

With enough miles logged in, you can see from the record what will happen to these children in flight. To predict their future, all you need is to complete the log. We've already looked at this educational movement's failed test of experience. Now let's look at the failed test of research.

At a drug fair, Nata Preis told Coulson about Project SMART, an experimental alcohol education program at the University of Southern California. This "personhood model" stressed decision making and self-esteem for children. It held that "to become your own person" is the best guarantee for healthy living, even for children.

On conducting scheduled followup research, however, she and her colleagues found significantly more members of the experimental group than the controls imbibed alcohol. "It was as if we had driven them to drink!" she said.

Afterwards the researchers returned to repair the damage from the experimental induction. "It took a couple of years," she said, "but most of the kids have now returned to normal. Yet when I tell other drug educators about our earlier results, their mouths fall open. They can't believe it. In fact, they *won't.*" In drug education circles, it is contrary to faith to question the value of kids deciding things for themselves.[2]

This is the kind of unwavering faith educators exhibited in 1975 when results came in on another feeling-centered, program. In that year at Stanford University, psychologist Richard H. Blum and his research team completed data analysis on DECIDE and in 1976 published results in *Drug Education: Results and Recommendations.*

To set up the independent variable in his experiment, the Stanford psychologist chose discussion groups employing values clarification and decision making with emphasis on personal, interactional, and affective components. Of the 1586 elementary, junior high, and high school students, 991 "experimentals" participated in therapeutic exercises and discussions; the other 595 students were the control group, who received no treatment. To the surprise of Blum and his colleagues, those receiving affective education used alcohol, tobacco, and marijuana *sooner* than the control students. And they used drugs *more extensively* than the untreated. This outcome countered all expectations.

To check those results, Blum and his team did another test in 1978, this time with 1413 new sixth grade subjects. But results were the same: more drug use by the experimental group than the control group.

Later, taking his scientific caution with him, Blum long ago withdrew from DECIDE. Other program promoters should have dropped out, too, Coulson says, because these studies at the outset showed that this approach misfires in the classroom. But DECIDE and programs like it continue anyway.[3]

Thomas Gordon was another who admitted his method failed the test of results, in at least four areas. A protege of Carl Rogers, Gordon wrote about communication skills, conflict resolution, and decision making. And yet he admitted his approach did not eliminate or postpone smoking, premarital sex, marijuana use, and neglecting homework.

Like many promoters, even with failure Gordon did not become discouraged with his methods. Rather he taught parents how to live with the consequences of his kind of teaching. "It is understandable," he writes, "that many parents feel so strongly about certain behaviors that they do not want to give up trying to influence their children, but a more objective view usually convinces them that they have no other feasible alternative except to give up—to accept what they cannot change." "I often tell parents," he adds, "Don't want your child to become something in particular; just want him to become."

Research suggests that one cause of Gordon's failure is his principle that teachers and parents must not lecture. According to a study by Judith Brook, M.D. and Douglas Wilson, M.D., this is bad advice for those who want to prevent children from smoking.

Researchers Brook and Wilson, in the mid 1980s, studied the qualities and strategies of the relationship between fathers and sons, comparing youngsters who smoked to those who did not. Whether fathers smoked was not significant, either as a main effect or an interaction. What mattered was that fathers who prevented their sons from smoking talked about their intolerance of tobacco and marijuana use. They had "high expectations for their sons" to heed their advice. Significantly, the deterring factors—expressed intolerance, high expectations, or lecturing—are not present in decision making programs.

Another study by Wilson and another team also proves false the principle that repeated lecturing does harm, not good. In this study, of the 211 patients counseled to stop smoking, 106 received follow-up sessions, whereas the 105 in the control group did not. Follow up sessions compare to "lecturing" or repetitive "preaching" by teachers or parents. Overall, twenty-three percent in the lectured experimental group quit smoking and only twelve percent in the not-lectured control group quit. . . And among those who smoked regular-tar cigarettes, the proportion of patients who quit smoking was about five times as great in the experimental group as in the control group. These tallies came from reports six to twelve months after entry into the trial.

What differentiated the successful stop-smoking group from the failed one? Telling the participant, "Don't smoke," not once but many times. And yet direct intervention is the kind of activity decision making education outlaws. Children are supposed "to decide for themselves."[4]

Because research consistently shows failure, decision making programs often continue without conducting objective research on resulting behavior, in some cases for years. In 1989, however, Bainbridge Island schools broke the educational movement's period of research silence by testing the results of Here's Looking at You, a program by Clay Roberts.

With the following quoted one-liners, the front page of the November 11, 1989 Wall Street Journal reported on the program in this affluent suburb near Seattle: On a Friday a youngster on the run yelled, "It's time for some D&A"—drugs and alcohol. "Drugs are as plentiful as potato chips," said graduate Keith Winfield. "I drink and get high because it's fun," said senior Abe Golden. Another said she got her high from straight liquor. "In Bainbridge, students study hard and party hard." she added.

"Bainbridge is just like many high schools across the country, substance-abuse experts say, except for one alarming respect: For twelve years, Bainbridge schools have run one of the most intensive and innovative anti-drug education programs in the country," the item says.

Instruction begins in first grade with emphasis on self-esteem for two years. From third to twelfth, students write essays on drugs, role-play, and engage in group sessions with emphasis again on self-esteem.

In spite of this intensive training, the article says that informal polling reveals that five percent of secondary students are chemically dependent. And as many as seventy percent use drugs or alcohol weekly, says Catherine Camp, a teacher on the Island. "We went into this study hoping to find positive results. But the data proved to the contrary," says Armand Mauss, a Washington State University professor, who has studied the Bainbridge program.

"It would give me great pride to say that we've done this for twelve years and it's really working," Julia Wan, assistant superintendent of schools, says. "But that's not the case."

The district will continue with an updated version of the same program—Here's Looking at You 2000. This newer program has an even "stronger social skills component," author Roberts says. "It teaches kids how to be assertive; how to control their own behavior; how to make new friends, and how to help friends who are in trouble. It also emphasizes the need for kids to get bonded to pro-social institutions like the Boy Scouts, a church group, or a community organization of sorts," he points out. The program also exhorts parents to get involved.[5]

How successful the updated program will be remains to be seen. You will see in a study cited later that although change brings restraint and improvements to programs, nevertheless, damage will continue unless the harmful base for the program disappears. With the base gone, however, there is no reason for the program to exist.[6]

Another tested area of humanistic programs is sex education. The fact is that several studies in recent years have established that sex education itself, as the public school typically structures it, contributes to early onset of sexual activity. This research shows that students in the experimental group increase in sexual activity and begin earlier than students from the control group. In one study, the record stands even though Planned Parenthood would have wanted to be able to point to good results. But once again, scientific findings, this time by Marsiglio and Mott, proved that increased dangerous activity results from decision making education. Look for the data on pages 151 to 162 in the Summer 1986 issue of *Family Planning Perspectives* published by Alan Guttmacher Institute, an affiliate of Planned Parenthood.

It's a significant study because of its scale: 12,000 young people in a national representative sample. This means that we can have a fair degree of confidence in generalizing from the sample to the population of youngsters at large. Also, as for reliability, Table 8 on page 159 reveals that with respect to the four co-factors, the findings reach the ".01 level of significance." What that means is that there is less than one chance in a hundred that the reading will turn out to be mistaken about how things really are.

The editors are not able to gloss over the results because scientists Marsiglio and Mott, committed to truth telling, can't hide the fact that "prior exposure to a sex education course is positively and significantly associated with the initiation of sexual activity at ages 15 and 16" (page 158).

Researchers, Marsiglio and Mott, looked for factors that affect sexual activity in children; they cited four co-factors:

1 - children of some racial backgrounds less apt to be sexually active
2 - children of church going parents less apt to be sexually active
3 - children of more highly educated parents less likely to be sexually active
4 - children who have sex education more apt to be sexually active

The last co-factor is the only one over which parents have control. They cannot change their race; they cannot suddenly have a diploma or instantly build a record of many years of church attendance. But they can keep their children out of current, affective sex education courses.[7]

Other research shows that peer-group process education seems custom designed to harm good children. See "A Study of Cigarette Smoking among Teenage Girls and Young Women," an unpublished research report for the American Cancer Society by Yankelovich, Skelly, White. Yankelovich's study shows that for students who reach conclusions about values amongst themselves and practice "unconditional understanding" and "nonjudgmentalism," the direction of influence flows from experienced to inexperienced.

Yankelovich dispels the notion that a socially ill-at-ease youngster turns to cigarettes as a means of being thought of as more sophisticated or as a needed prop for handling social situations. He says, on the contrary, child-smokers are more socially aggressive and have the power to influence classmates. In a decision making class, the users have influence that they would not otherwise have because abstainers do not ordinarily choose drug or tobacco users in their natural circle of friends.

The study shows that those girls who won't smoke are more timid socially; they are happy in their trusting relationship with their parents and do not feel the need nor do they want to pose as adults. They are the conscientious ones who listen to their teachers, take notes, and learn.

Placed in circles with smoker-peers for value clarification, these students continue in the same spirit of cooperation. Because they are in the circle groups at the direction of their teachers, they listen, take mental notes, and learn, but what they learn is to their harm.

"It is the teenage girl nonsmoker who tends to be quieter, have less self-confidence, or self esteem, and is shy with the boys." That's the way the report describes the girl nonsmoker who, through classroom peer-interaction, is led into experimentation in a hazardous lifestyle. This girl is fruit on the vine, ready to be plucked.

In the past such a girl formerly looked to her parents or God as her guide, but under the influence of nondirective teaching, she no longer considers this guidance adequate. She learns to subjectivize morals; that is, she learns that no standard of right or wrong is quite as adequate as thoughtfully *deciding* what to do. Indeed, from this exposure she learns that the only *moral* path is to make up her own mind.[8]

REACTIONS TO FAILURE

All the studies confirm what the research team under Carl Rogers learned about affective education. Although their experience did not apply to drug or sex education, all the experiments were similar in several ways: The process methods were alike, results were universally disconcerting, and team members were equally unwilling to accept the findings. As humanistic psychologists, the programs had sounded so right. That's why they couldn't believe the research.

In the educational establishment, Rogers encountered what his therapeutic model overlooked: real-life politics. He claimed that because his experiments had begun to thrive, politics resisted the forward move. He summed up his frustration by saying that society believes in a hierarchical form of organization, with a leader at the top and authority delegated down. To challenge this *given* is to threaten "a way of being that is deeply rooted in our society," he said. And his philosophy does threaten the usual educational structure, for it advocates relationships on equal footing, horizontal rather than vertical.

The impracticality of this approach in educational relationships shows up in the reaction to failure by one client-centered therapist. When asked how he could so roundly condemn all educators, he said he felt that way because these people were not his clients. If they were, he said he could feel warmly. The truth is that the politics of his relationship to educators does not correspond to therapy. For therapy is a contract between two persons, one of whom can suspend belief in ordinary relationship to enter into a professional, therapeutic one. Under the artificiality of this agreement, near-miracles are possible. But there is no evidence that such agreements are possible, or even desirable, in real life situations. And yet the foundation principle of person-centered education sets up the therapeutic relationship to be the model for children to follow in all of real life.[9]

What makes possible this blind disregard for reality? The human longing for perfection, for Utopia, which Maslow at one time aspired to and later forsook; he called it Eupsychia. Following a phantom goal results in two things. First, to take a worthy but limited theory and apply it to life wholesale, without boundaries, is to court disaster. Some school projects, like the Immaculate Heart program, go into high gear, then crash to a halt; others like Bainbridge Island continue for years. For schools, a crash is disruptive, and a long continuous program is expensive and disappointing. But for individual lives within the decision making programs, harm can be both catastrophic and long lasting.

Second, to claim that universal therapeutic practice encompasses all issues trivializes other values. Philosopher and scientist Michael Polanyi said that official devotion to isolated ideals destroys them. "Such a society would to some degree become ossified into a rigid set of meaningless objectives," he said.[10]

From the days of Carl Rogers to the present, the findings of research continue to reveal the same results. And many now in control of education continue to ignore results; to them the movement remains attractive. Although schoolboards and administrators tell children in their programs, "Consider the consequences of the choices you make," these leaders refuse to acknowledge the consequences of the programs they push.

THREE QUESTIONS ABOUT FAILED PROGRAMS

In discussing these failed programs, I will consider three questions. The first one: *Is it not possible that changes in execution of the same program might bring good instead of harmful results?* As a matter of fact, Coulson found a difference in one classroom in the *Growing Healthy* program. The teacher had control of the class, and it was clear that students appreciated that. They'd done their homework. They gave sharp answers and asked relevant questions, and when they didn't, the teacher let them know about it. As an observer Coulson could read the message students conveyed to their teacher: "Thanks for not coddling us.

Thanks for holding us to account. We know this drug education is serious business. We know that lives are at stake." The session was definitely *not* a simulated psychotherapy session.

BUT. . . When Coulson commented on her academic approach, the staff assumed that because he was a psychologist, he was unhappy with the teacher's performance—that he expected her to create a more feeling-centered classroom environment. They couldn't imagine that he admired the teacher's commanding delivery, which turned out to be in violation of the program's guide. Improvements noted in other programs, too, were largely accidental or off the stated norm!.

Although this particular program does well to include factual study of physical and biological principles, the teacher's guide warns against becoming too academic. "Exciting" is the favored word. "One of the most notable features is the elimination of the stereotypical 'directive-authoritarian' role of the teacher," the handbook states about the program. Could it be that the handbook's photograph of a teacher scratching his head best illustrates the kind of teacher the program commends?[11]

In discussing these failed programs, I now ask the second question: *Is it not possible that the affective programs themselves can be modified to gain good results?* Let's answer that by looking at results in studies by Richard Blum. The 1976 study used a *nondirective mode* (called Z, group discussion); the 1978 study employed *the original nondirective mode* (labeled Z, group discussion) and a *modified nondirective mode* (labeled C, group discussion plus some instruction).

The studies, however, yielded the same results, namely "quicker and wider use of alcohol, tobacco, and cannabis [marijuana]." Even with modification of the program, results were negative.

My conclusion is that a false base renders lesser improvements futile.

In discussing these failed programs, I now ask the third question: *Does this kind of education have any positive results that show up in research findings?* There are no assurances, only inconsistent possibilities: For students already using drugs, the study seems to indicate that this drug education *might* slow them from expanding drug use to more or harder drugs.

BUT for nonusing, well reared children, results in other research have been consistently negative. These kids are more likely to remain abstinent without decision making drug education. On page 380 of his report, Blum notes that for nonusers, the effect of this kind of drug education is "to speed the uptake of use of the popular compounds, alcohol, tobacco, and cannabis."

"We adhere to the general recommendation offered in *Drug Education: Results and Recommendations*. Where children's exposure to drugs is minimal. . . do not engage in school-based drug education per se." In this statement Blum repeated his 1976 recommendation on page 423.

The bypassing of this kind of instruction is imperative when the proposed mode of drug education favors the kind of education discussed in this book or even modified forms of it. To teach drug education where drug exposure is minimal is to democratize the classroom—but at the price of sacrificing well-reared youngsters to drug use for the sake of *possibly* helping users slow down expansion to hard drugs. The repeated outcome is that where a few may have had drug problems to begin with, more have drug problems after completion of the programs.[12]

CONCLUSIONS

For children who would otherwise live drug-free lives, drug education by peer-group activity is bad news. For troubled youngsters, classroom psychotherapy is not powerful enough; they need professional help. Nevertheless, enthusiastic educators disregard the facts, intrude into private lives, and condemn non-enthusiasts as enemies of balanced psychological development. Professionals in the field of psychology, however, know better; they are waking up to this danger because some of their patients are casualties of nondirective education.

The basic point that schools miss is that the classroom task is much different from the therapeutic, Coulson says. To fail to recognize this is to put good children at risk. With mandatory public schooling, we need to be more concerned about children whom schools damage—those who otherwise would steer a straight course. These are the minor children whose ideas about home authority and other beliefs these school programs violate.

We need to stop focusing all our attention on a small minority of students who refuse to listen to instruction and advice, says Coulson. And conversely we have to give the good influences in our society the right to exist.

"Thus while I argue against formal drug education for low risk children, I advocate powerful parental involvement" in the lives of children, says Coulson. Family life that transmits values and controls can successfully reduce drug risks—*especially careful supervision of children with respect to their peer associations,"* he adds.

Such parental control, of course, is precisely what feeling-oriented drug education cancels because neither parents nor children select classroom conversation partners or topics to be discussed. Circle groups amount to school-arranged friendship. Such, in fact, is their misdirected, egalitarian purpose.

With repeated, negative results, psychotherapeutic program executors abandon research; statistics can run them out of business. Now program pushers favor subjective evaluation; they point to "improved" attitudes and factual gains. But is that enough? "Children who have had such education have better *attitudes* toward drugs," a foreign father, a doctoral candidate in the States, observed. "They have more accurate *knowledge* about drugs, *BUT* they are *more likely to use* drugs. . . I believe that drug education should *sell* sobriety rather than promote a process of decision making."[13]

At the conclusion of this log, let's ask what it is that keeps self-esteem programs in flight. Without rational justification, only exuberance sparks the last functioning engine. These nondirected flights are like that of a 1989 aircraft that continued flying for a thousand miles with a dead pilot slumped over the controls. All that accompanying air force planes could do was follow the runaway, ready to shoot it down if necessary to save a populated area.

Coulson sums up the matter in words like these: We can't afford to kid ourselves. *Decision making education is deadly.* It's not working. I defy anyone to show me research that children are better off than before. No one can.[14]

4 IF THIS DOESN'T WORK, WHO PUSHES IT?

Carl Rogers was the first influential pusher of nondirective education.

Although Coulson learned from Rogers what he *said* about nondirectiveness, Coulson considers himself more indebted to his mentor for what he *did*. Coulson appreciates what he learned about discipline and conduct through daily exposure to the man himself.

When a team member suggested that Rogers write about discipline, he said, "I can't. Discipline to me is like water to a fish. It's my element. I can't see it." Therefore, because he couldn't see it, Rogers felt he couldn't write about it, but neither did he place value upon it in his teaching.

His disciplined example seems to contradict what he taught; and to Coulson it conveys a powerful message. In family life, he learned the wisdom of intervention by Rogers in earlier days to pressure his son to excel and to go to medical school. And in his professional life, Coulson learned that if you want to make an impact on the world, then you'd better go out and do it. That's what he tries to do when he lectures about the dangers of psychotherapy in the classroom and about the exploitation of those who push it. In this respect—in seeking to influence those who will listen—Coulson follows the example, not the teaching, of Rogers.[1]

EDUCATIONAL AND FINANCIAL INTERESTS WHO PUSH

Of those groups in education and commerce who push this education that harms children, I name five groups.

Psychologists, the first group, introduced psychotherapy into the classroom. Rogers and his colleagues proposed this approach for education because they thought they'd made a wonderful discovery. But after the person-centered approach failed, why did they keep pushing it?

Rogers explained what motivated him. He didn't forge ahead to gain position or honors; he wanted to make an impact, he himself said in a 1976 public television interview. That craving for influence over many people's lives is probably what led him to extend his theory excessively. Freud did the same thing; he could explain everything. Everything.[2] This overreaching is the stuff from which emerges ideology.

Earlier in the fifties Abraham Maslow claimed ideological territory for psychology. "I think psychologists are the most important people living today," Maslow wrote in 1956. "I think the fate of the human species and the future of the human species rests more upon their shoulders than upon any group of people now living. I believe that all the important problems of war and peace, exploitation and brotherhood. . . the happiness and unhappiness of mankind will yield only to a better understanding of human nature." He went so far as to call humanistic psychology *psychosalvationism* but later retracted such sweeping claims.[3]

In this psychotherapeutic ideology, humanists find a home; they make up a second group of pushers of Rogerian education.

John Dewey was one early humanist in American education. This philosopher, psychologist, and educator propelled progressive education into the twentieth century. He emphasized learning through experimentation and opposed authoritarian methods.

In 1933 as principal author of *Humanist Manifesto I*, he defined humanism: "Religious humanists regard the universe as self-existing and not created. . . Humanism believes that man is a part of nature and that he has emerged as the result of a continuous process. . . Humanists are firmly convinced that existing acquisitive and profit-motivated society has shown itself to be inadequate and that a *radical* change in methods, controls, and motives must be instituted (emphasis added)."[4]

"The teacher is the true prophet of God and the usherer in of the kingdom of God," Dewey once stated.

Humanist Manifesto II is the latest formal statement on humanism. It attacks the Judeo and Christian faiths by saying that humanists "believe that traditional theism, especially faith in the prayer-hearing god. . . is an unproved and outmoded faith. Salvationism based on mere affirmation, still appears as harmful, diverting people with false hopes of heaven hereafter. . . No deity will save us; we must save ourselves.

"We affirm that moral values derive their source from human experience. Ethics is autonomous and situational, needing no theological or ideological sanction. . .

"We look to the development of a system of world law and a world order based on transnational federal government."[5]

For this updated humanist statement, Allen Guttmacher, President of Planned Parenthood, was one of many, influential signers.

About the humanist system of beliefs, Professor Harvey Cox in his book, *The Secular City*, writes about "secularism," which he says "is the name for an ideology, a new closed worldview which functions very much like a new religion." He says that although the secular state now grants freedom of religion, it learned that concept from biblical faith. And he warns that secularism threatens freedom and must be watched "to prevent its becoming the ideology of a new establishment," which seeks to impose its ideology through government.[6]

Educators make up a third group that pushes this education. The same desire for influence that prompts psychologists also makes educators push this way of life. And so, closing their eyes to reality and research, pushers recommend psychotherapy to *all* children, no matter the quality of their family life. They justify the coercive use of the power of the State because of the "necessity" to make students "better"—in spite of the wishes, beliefs, and practices of their families.

About this pushing of decision making education, Blum wrote in mid 1970 the following: "The considerable materials which propose what [it] ought to do are not matched by an equal volume of information describing what happens in or as a consequence of doing it." The same way to operate prevails today, and self-esteem programs multiply.

Working together with the educational hierarchy for humanistic education is the fourth group, the leadership of teachers' unions. Two of them are the National Education Association (NEA) and the American Federation of Teachers (AFT). The NEA has lobbied a humanistic agenda for years. And Albert Shanker, president of the AFT, exerts a lot of influence in Washington, D.C.[7] Although leaders do not necessarily express the will of individual teachers, or even the majority of them, they speak in their behalf.

These unions join with educators in the larger world of politics to create one of the biggest lobbies in the country. For example, in one district alone, Northern California Congresswoman Barbara Boxer received from the NEA $25,500, her largest PAC campaign donation over six years.[8] In fact, the power of these groups has so surged that education has become the focus itself of lobbying by other groups that have financial and political interests. And that leads us to the next group.

Financial interests make up the fifth group that pushes education that harms children.

Publishers and creators of self-esteem programs make up one part of this financial interest group. Their training and materials are universally expensive.

Others have commercial motives that are not so obvious. With their marketing aims, other lobbies make handy co-pushers with humanists in education. In one of the largest campaigns to influence public thinking, the National Association of State Boards of Education (NASBE) teams up with the Tobacco Institute to sponsor the free public service booklets, *Helping Youth Decide* and *Helping Youth Say No*. Together education and industry, in the name of better parent/child communication, promote principles that condition parents to accept decision making education as a way of life. Although the NASBE claims it doesn't endorse the tobacco product, what does it matter if the Tobacco Institute endorses the school product—children! That's their targeted market.[9]

The NASBE furnishes their endorsement and distributes the *Helping Youth* booklets. The Tobacco Institute produces the publications and picks up the bill, which is staggering. At one point the Institute had paid for more than eighty-one million separate advertising impressions for *Helping Youth Decide;* and some of these ads were full page ones in *Time, Newsweek,* and other magazines. Add to that the expense of the four-color, glossy, high-quality paper and printing job for the illustrated booklets.[10]

This continuing advertising blitz has not been without repercussions, however. Former Surgeon General C. Everett Koop, overseer of the nation's health, kept a running battle with these sponsors because he knew something about nondirective education and its consequences. About such exploitation, Edwin J. DeLattre, at that time in the U.S. Department of Education, also complained that "children are invited to a world where it is a travesty and an imposition for anyone to tell them the truth."[11]

Coulson himself knows something about the educational lobby. In 1988 after he became a member of the Federal Drug Education Curriculum Panel, the tobacco interest R. J. Reynolds Nabisco pressured him. Coulson had published a review paper critical of affective drug education. Because of this, a senior Quest official tried to get Coulson to believe he was insufficiently nonjudgmental, not very Rogerian. Pressure increased as the date for the second meeting of the panel approached.[12]

This cigarette manufacturer, R. J. Reynolds Nabisco, a major packager of drug education curricula, sponsors Quest. It funds with hundreds of thousands of dollars this program, which serves primary, junior high, and high school levels: *Skills for Living, Skills for Growing, Skills for Adolesence*. Without financial interest groups like these, educators would be unable to continue their nondirective programs.

As profit making enterprises, cigarette companies unfailingly act according to their interests. They do not support programs that will hurt them. Nothing in today's anti-smoking climate, of course, changes that. It only makes them more alert to opportunity. Therefore, now that the adult world has become a resistant market, cigarette companies more than ever must sell to children. The fact is that ninety percent of today's adults who buy cigarettes became addicted in childhood. Logically, therefore, an education campaign makes sense. Do their tactics work? Yes, compared to a decade ago, ten times as many twelve year old girls smoke today.[13]

The former Surgeon General has noted that "the seduction of young people is the very essence of survival for the Tobacco Institute and the cigarette manufacturing industry." The industry needs new smokers, Koop says, because many who started smoking as teenagers will die this year.[14]

Therefore, children, for their good, need to know how to turn away from the seductiveness of tobacco advertising. They don't need to learn the decision making formula. Nor do they need to be told to turn within to seek out their desires. For what do they find as their desire when they turn within? The desire to belong to a group. And who dominates the "magic circle" discussion in the classroom? The smokers. These are the experienced ones who have something to share.[15]

In another area, sex education, it's not surprising that those who push these nondirective programs also come from financial interest groups; pharmaceutical companies and clinics invest in developing a market for their birth control products and abortion services.

In 1987 the Ortho Pharmaceutical Company distributed almost 4000 free sex education curriculum kits to high schools throughout the country. You can call their 800 hot line and ask them, "What about abstinence? Are you going to teach abstinence?" They'll say, "Oh, yes. We cover that, too." But they can't cover it very well. Given the bottom line of their corporation, the motivation remains suspect. Ortho doesn't make a profit from abstinence.[16]

Nor does Planned Parenthood, an organization in the birth control and abortion business. (If you've been led to believe that Planned Parenthood doesn't do abortions, look under *birth control* in the yellow pages to find their abortion services [if the group services your area].) With the high failure rate of condoms, teaching "safe sex" is good for their abortion business. In order to receive government grants and to make its profits,

Planned Parenthood has to have a reason for its existence; that reason is sexually active young people in need of contraceptives and abortion.

ETR Associates, which furnishes schools much of the material used in sex education classes today, also promotes the goals of Planned Parenthood.

Ortho's sex education program, Straight Talk, carries a "primary message" about abstinence, a public relations man told Coulson, but none of Coulson's neighbors could find that message in the program's video they watched. A doctor in the presentation tells the children, "You're told you can't vote until you're eighteen. And in many states, you're told you can't drink until you're twenty-one. But the decision to have sex is your own, and it's an adult one. That means that you, and not anyone else, can decide when you're ready for sex." On hearing this, one of Coulson's neighbors hit the television pause button. "Is he saying, 'You're ready for sex if you *say* you are'?" she asked. "It sounds that way," her husband answered. Children are too young to vote, too young to drink, but not too young to decide to have sex, the film implies.

In only fifty seconds, the "abstinence" portion, of the video told the children they *could* postpone sex. The tone of this addendum was, "That's okay, too."

The instruction booklet for the teacher was no better: "Ideally, your role in the discussion should be minimal. We suggest that you appoint a student discussion leader from your class to conduct the talk."

Contemporary Ob/Gyn, November 1988, reveals the purpose of Ortho's recommendation for peer-leadership in discussions: An article suggests that teachers "involve adolescents in peer-group discussions" because the authors have found students more responsive to their peers than to others about contraception.

It's clear, in general, that peers promote dubious schemes and products more confidently than teachers do.[17] Therefore, sexual experimentation also is more likely to follow when peers lead. For although the teacher stays aware of community standards in what she can say or do, peers are less likely to feel that responsibility. And with students leading, the teacher feels relieved of accountability.

The growing purchasing power of children is something else that makes corporations find their way into the field of education. Witness again the entrance of the Robert Wood Johnson Foundation, this time into the school-based clinic movement. Ortho benefits from decision making sex education courses, not only in sales for Ortho but in customers for the school clinics. With greater profits for Ortho, the more money will the Johnson Foundation have to promote still more school-based clinics.[18]

All that these supplying industries need is the opportunity to present abstinence as a matter of choice, as one alternative to dangerous behavior: drugs *or* alternatives, smoking *or* alternatives, sex *or* alternatives. Then to make cash registers ring, peer influence and advertising will do the rest.

POLITICAL, RELIGIOUS, IDEOLOGICAL ACTIVISTS WHO PUSH

Behind affective education lies a philosophy that a number of groups push. These are political, religious, and ideological activists, of which I will name five more groups.

One of these, a sixth group, pushes self-esteem as the answer for all social ills. The Self-Esteem Task Force Commission of the State of California is one example. It pushes affective, decision making education in the schools and elsewhere. Similar task forces are popping up in California counties, in the state of Maryland, and in other states. And through these groups funded by taxes, education that harms children gains favor.

The seventh group combines politics, social issues, and religion. In the churches as in the schools and unions, ideologues gain places of prestige and power in order to push their ideas within the organization and to the community beyond. They do this in spite of differing values the laity may hold. For the sad fact is that parochial schools and congregations fall under the same psychologizing influences as public education. None are exempt; Catholics, protestants, or Jews.

The laity often fails to recognize what is happening, especially in the early stages. Abraham Maslow spoke of the welcome he received when he spoke before religious institutions. "They shouldn't applaud me—they should attack. If they were fully aware of what I was doing, they would," he wrote on April 17, 1962 in his journal after a very successful lecture that night before hundreds of Catholics.

Many within this seventh group are New Agers, who combine religion with politics. In the schools they encourage the teaching of "peace and justice," "one world government," and "globalism." By globalism in the schools, I do not refer to study of foreign cultures, history, and government; those subjects are adequately provided for in the academic curriculum of schools. I am referring to the globalistic worldview that has a Marxist slant combined with an anti-American bias.

Beyond War, a network of projects, and Peace the 21st are two examples of New Age groups that sometimes work within the schools. (If you were unaware that these groups are New Age, you can find them listed in networks of New Age groups. In keeping with peaceful times, however, they will probably change their names.) They agree with the objectives of humanistic education, including the guided meditations, relaxation techniques, the emphasis on North American, Celtic, Eastern religions, and the earth religions.

Advocates of liberation theology make up another group in this category that endorses the decision making way of life, especially globalism. They push their own agenda in seminaries, churches, and wherever they can, including the schools.

The eighth group of pushers are those with "alternate lifestyles"— homosexuals, pornographers, militant feminists. This group has a strong, vocal political base and lobbying power in education. Under the guise of teaching about AIDS, they achieve status with the young and promote their behavior.

The ninth group, the media, is powerful on both the national and local level in shaping the future of schools. Generally, the media supports promoters of the person-centered approach to life. This shows up in many ways in "news reporting." Readers often fail to notice subtle bias or distortion in news reports—for a very small example, the reporting of the former Surgeon General's comments at Liberty College. "The ideal is chastity, monogamy, and marriage," Koop told his Christian listeners there. But how did the Washington Post quote him? "The ideal [for you] is chastity, monogamy, and marriage."

The revised version differs from what Mr. Koop expressed. Did the public recognize this? Or are we so steeped in "I have my experience and you have yours" that we miss the change in meaning?[19]

The tenth group of pushers of decision making education gives legal aid and media promotion to the ideals of the person-centered approach. Two specific groups—the American Civil Liberties Union and People for the American Way—have good titles but a partisan stance. Both have money, political power, and a network of followers through which they exert tremendous influence. Through mass mailings and through his television programs, Norman Lear, founder of People for the American Way can sway huge audiences.

ROADBLOCKS TO RESISTANCE AGAINST
PUSHERS OF EDUCATION THAT HARMS

For those who see the dangers, why is it so difficult to oppose this movement? There's an answer to this puzzle. In the person-centered approach, in which feelings preempt reason, criticism can find no forum for expression. To reduce all differing opinions to the level of differences of taste allows no ground for resolution of conflict. Also, for anyone to criticize the approach is to confirm the built-in theory of psychology that opponents "practice resistance."[20]

Another problem in opposing this movement is that with youth's natural bent for rebellion and with built-in peer pressure to throw off moral restraint, students become natural allies of the humanist establishment. Because today's process education ignores reality and concentrates on how students feel about themselves, the programs throw students back on their own devices. Coulson's conclusion after personal and extensive surveying of these programs is that the most likely outcome of their influence is for children to fall away from the absolutes of their parents and the teachings of their religious faith. Thus, with educators and peers, the child joins hands against his family and his heritage.

I think that parents and citizens are also pushers of this kind of education—some because they share the same philosophy, but most by default, by failing to speak out. Silence on matters of such grave importance communicates tacit approval. In fact, this ideology now so grips our society that those with differing views from humanism accept a back seat without question. A parent in 1989 called in to Coulson's interview on a radio talk-show to ask, "Do I have the right to say, 'No, my kid is not going to talk to the guidance counselor'?"

Of course parents have rights over their minor children. "We taxpayers built the school system," Coulson answered, "and then we act as if the system is our boss and we are the employees. We feel like knuckleheads if we say anything. The hangup comes because teachers and counselors are supposed to have better knowledge than parents about child behavior. And parents don't like to be considered pushy by resisting what the schools do." Nevertheless, the Hatch Amendment gives parents the right to prohibit psychological experimentation on students in national programs. And for other rights, parents have the constitution to back them up.[21]

As a consequence of our abandoning common sense, parents and teachers rein themselves in from active responsibility for the young. But peers, advertisers, political and financial interest groups, and dealers do not hesitate to rush into the vacuum we've left behind; they become the ones to shape the lives of children, Coulson says. While affective education institutionalizes adult timidity, exploiters wax bold.

This should not be. "Parents *must* tell their children what to do," Coulson writes. "It's a horrible mistake to tell youngsters they must make up their own minds about important matters. We must say, 'Yeah, make up your own mind but by all means make it up in the right way.'"

Does this conclusion sound too simple? Coulson did not arrive at it quickly or easily. Like the rest of us, he tried for a time to tune out warning bells because to pay attention means to face obligation head on. But think about this: Unless someone stands against them, exploiters will continue to push education that harms children.

5 WHY DOES THIS EDUCATION CAUSE HARM?

Why does this education cause harm? Let me name the ways.

This education harms children because it does not make distinctions: It does not distinguish adults from children nor the clinic from the classroom.[1] *In the clinic, nondirective group therapy for adults yields benefits. In the classroom, the same approach for children can devastate.*

The history of psychotherapy has been to find ways to encourage patients or clients to talk freely. For without this openness the patient's defenses remain in control, and neither the doctor nor the patient can know the real problem. Freud was the first to struggle with achieving this goal. He tried hypnotizing and even bullying before he hit upon his cardinal rule of free association: "I will never censor you—nor must you censor yourself when we are together."

In the client-centered approach of Rogers, a group therapist's aim is to draw out the clients, to create a climate of safety, to help clients identify their feelings. For the group leader knows that if he throws out quick and insistently authoritative answers, he can forestall cures. Instead, he creates an environment to insure thorough personal exploration. Often, especially in the early weeks of a newly formed group, the therapist may also have to prevent group members themselves from offering solutions. Jumping in to offer solutions to an individual who is just beginning to engage in personal exploration delays necessary *further* exploration. What is unique about therapy is that this nondirective exploration is in the inner life, the subjective realm of experience.[2]

The child, in contrast to the adult, has not yet developed his "self", and his needs are different, Coulson says. The child has not built up a reservoir of experience to explore. He needs the benefit of adult experience; he needs the security of adult direction to guide him as he grows. Therefore, if he is saddled with decisions that require judgment and maturity and does not receive the necessary adult support, he caves in to outside pressures. To remove authoritative foundations from the student's life puts him at risk.

John Dewey earlier cast the child as scientist. This recent humanistic movement wrecks this "scientist's" lab and cripples scientific trailblazing capabilities. "For it must be said that the world is so constructed that children *cannot* prosper in it by their own lights," says Coulson. Children are not adults; they need responsible adults in their lives.[3]

This education harms children because it places roadblocks between parent and child and undermines the authority of the home. Although it claims to be value neutral, it has an agenda of its own.

"You must decide for yourself which role to adopt," a text author tells the pupil. "A major influence on you has been the attitudes and behaviors of each of your parents. . . You have probably learned some fairly traditional ideas. . . Many people believe that these traditional attitudes hinder growth and development of a person because they limit possibilities. . . Only you can judge."[4]

It is wrong for this text and for schools "to assume that parents by nature oppress offspring and that only classroom therapy can set children free," says Coulson. To alienate children from parents doesn't mean they're going to make free choices. Rather, they're going to make choices that are popular, that peer groups enforce, and that dealers promote. The humanistic classroom has become a mainline route to loss of freedom.

When the school attacks the home's belief system, it intrudes into a child's private life and violates his parents' rights. It pushes the child off solid ground, throws him into troubled waters beyond his depth, and shouts, "Build your own reality!" And a very unreliable reality it is, because if the child creates it, he can change it as well. And if he learns to see one belief system as valid as another, isn't the best choice the path of least resistance? And doesn't that spell trouble, if not death by drowning in the sea of relativism?

In this classroom, the invulnerable student becomes vulnerable. The invulnerable is so named by researchers as most likely to avoid adolescent pitfalls; he is a church-goer, active in sports, scouts, and other activities. He is sincere and dutiful, typically the non-risktaker, the good child who loves parents and teachers and does not want to offend; he does his homework and takes to heart the lessons the school proposes.

This child, nurtured by influences of peer-group decision making, will give in to that which before he considered temptation, something to be resisted. Not only will his newly accepted behavior not be considered wrong, it will glow with allure; his teacher and his classmates will support him because he makes his "own decision."

The child learns to believe that rejection of his past leads to growth. In the process, however, lifelong defenses break down; he loses his fear of going against prohibitions of home and church. He's the innocent one this tested and failed human potential philosophy brings down.

The vision of the student will either be the vision of those who love him or of those who want to exploit him. Destroy parental authority for the child and he's an easy mark for the malevolent stranger.[5]

Program writers have an agenda of their own; they only appear to assume a neutral position above parochial intent. For once they announce their programs, or more accurately proclaim truth—particularly within the authoritative context society provides for professional opinion—they cannot maintain neutrality. They have no way to uphold a nondirective stance consistently except by silence. And that route is not one these "experts" will take, Coulson says, for they not only want to proclaim their method, they want all of society to embrace it. Humanistic program writers have their own values to convey.

Even in the matter of administering group work, a program writer sets up values by asking the teacher to lay out rules for "good listening," and "nonjudgmentalism." The teacher may reinforce this value judgment by asking the poor listener or judgmental student to leave the group activity. So what does the student learn? That doing the right thing in group work is important, but doing the right thing about drugs is a matter of choice. For educators to withhold authoritative teaching on anything other than rules for group therapy is to underestimate children's willingness to take instruction in matters of substance, Coulson says.

Value free programs are not and cannot be neutral about values. Silence by the teacher on important matters tells a student that a matter is debatable, unimportant, or that the teacher gives silent approval.

This education harms children because it allows children to make life and death decisions.

Topics in affective education are matters of importance. Most are, in fact, life and death issues. In matters of such serious consequence, to explore alternatives may be good group work with adults, but with students, it's foolhardy. In their formative years, they need guidance. Children ought not be deceived into believing that if they consult themselves, the world will tumble into line with their decisions.[6] Reality proves otherwise. Especially is it ridiculous for minor children *to explore* life threatening issues. The Neversmoke group uses an incident from the Harrison Ford movie, *Witness,* to illustrate.

In the film, Ford investigates a crime, suffers a bullet wound as a result, and ends up in the care of an Amish family. Still fearing for his safety, Ford keeps his loaded gun in a dresser drawer.

One day upon rising from his sick bed, Ford happens upon the family's young son indulging his eight year old curiosity; he's playing with the loaded gun.

How does Ford react? What if he took the decision making approach? "You have a right to your view of loaded guns, and I have a right to mine," he'd say. He'd ask the boy how he feels about what he is doing. He'd offer to teach him a six-step decision making process.

But that's not what Ford did in the movie, and that's not what you'd do in real life. "Never-*ever* play with a loaded gun!" Ford shouts. He speaks with the authority of an adult who has better judgment than a child. With the shout, Ford leads the boy through an exercise in kindness, an exercise in what I call single-trial learning. Urgency and danger dictate the only sensible way to react.

At the end, followup conversation between man and boy leaves no doubt that the boy has learned his lesson. He'll not forget what he must never-*ever* do.

This movie episode makes you face what common sense demands— that in the classroom life and death issues must be handled as life and death issues. With research to show us about the dangers of decision making education, we must not push children over the edge.

This education harms children because it works the wrong territory: The affective replaces the cognitive; that is, the subjective aims of the clinic replace the objective aims of the classroom. Also, by subjectivizing morals, this education violates the rights of pupils and parents. Furthermore, without objective standards, "self-esteem" programs cause academic decline, loss of self-esteem, and disrupted discipline.[7] The end result is that instead of equipping the child with knowledge and skills, this approach attempts to remake the personalities of students.

First, the obvious: Teachers are not psychotherapists. "[Being nondirective] seems and sounds so simple," Rogers said in a filmed interview in 1976. "It is actually *very difficult* to do." Experience and research teaches us that even when professional therapists oversee affective education for children, harm results. How much greater is the potential for danger with workshop trained teachers, who deal with guided imagery, hypnotic techniques of suggestion, and subjects like suicide![8]

The ways of the clinic and the classroom are incompatible because their aims differ; their realms are separate. The clinic offers what real life cannot—artificial conditions in a limited setting. In this unique professionally guided arrangement, the *voluntary* client can find fresh perspective without the fear of derailing his life. *He explores the inner reaches of his being.* The classroom, on the other hand, offers students instruction about the objective world. In this setting, the student learns knowledge and acquires skills for *living in the outside world.*

By abandoning objective standards and by bending reality to fit only present capabilities, "self-esteem" programs do children no favor. Conversely, requiring children to stretch *beyond themselves* according to objective standards challenges students to achieve and enables them to fulfill their potential.

In the psychotherapeutic focus "within," teacher and students turn their backs on the "beyond" of the outside world. And to do so confuses educational goals and weakens classroom performance. Then insofar as instructor and pupils act as if each individual creates his own reality, to that extent, each stops asking as much of the other. Thus, everyone fails to engage. And in practice no one becomes "the fully functioning person" Rogers portrayed.

I believe we are seeing such effects today. The consequence is not only decline in intellectual attainment but decline of morale as well—for with less expected of them and fewer challenges to meet, students have less reason to be proud of themselves; they lose the self-esteem that the programs claim to instill.[9]

This loss of self-esteem combined with familiarity bred by humanism's egalitarianism breaks down school discipline. In the sixties, a seventh grader at Immaculate Heart describes how frightened she and classmates were when the distance between teacher and pupil broke down. She says she lost respect for her teachers. At that time when fixed goals disappeared, besides loss of faith, literacy declined. That project bombed.

To justify the "self-esteem" philosophy, some say subjectivism and relativism are the only fair approach in America's pluralistic society. However, no matter how varied individual origins and beliefs, American heritage is one. And this shared political background accommodates differences by relegating values, religion, and politics to the private realm as *subjective* choices honored as freedoms by the State. For minor children, this subjective realm belongs to the family and to institutions of the parents' choice, tradition says. And for minor children, the objective realm of instruction belongs to the school, experience attests.

In our free society, subjective humanistic psychology cannot work in the classroom. After its transposition from the clinic, this subjective system violates the rights of public school children and their parents. Furthermore, subjectivism aborts the objective aims of education. When this happens, schools fail to teach adequately intellectual knowledge and useful skills. This abortion makes possible the intrusion into schools of the values, religious tenets, and political agendas of administrators or special interest groups. And with the public's lack of awareness of the switch from objective to subjective, these ideologies can intrude before anyone knows what's happening.

Take, for example, the subjectivism of affective drug education. Is the classroom the proper place to explore feelings about private values? "Does it matter what students feel about drugs any more than it matters what they feel about the alphabet? They need to learn the facts about drug use, not explore their feelings about drugs, and not investigate the attitudes and experience of user peers," Coulson says. There is a proper setting for *voluntary* exchange about feelings and attitudes and for discussion of values—including the humanistic way of life. For the *minor child,* that place is the home, church, synagogue, clinic, club, political group, or social organization—not the classroom.

In brief, classroom instruction should be to teach objective material with objective criteria for measurement. "It ought *not* be about remaking personality, for this cannot be done briefly, cannot be done by amateurs, and should not be done in school in any case," writes Coulson.[10]

But affective education does exactly what it should not; it recasts the student's identity. Role playing and group encounters make the student *subjective* about himself rather than objective. He becomes the center of his own feeling-centered world, no longer an obedient member of his family. And with the unspoken approval of the teacher—whom the invulnerable has learned from his parents to respect—he "clarifies" previously unrealized "values." He learns that he can become whatever he wants or "needs" to be. All he has to do is *decide.*

Under this induction, when he centers his attention on drugs, using is no longer something on the edge of his awareness. It is no longer in the realm of a report on the evening news. Drug use ceases to be personally unthinkable. It becomes an option.

"Energized" by one psychological classroom exercise after another, the student participates in heart to heart discussions with peers in the group-therapy circle. The nonuser discovers that classmate-users have emotions like his own; he learns to identify with the experienced. While submitting to that influence, the nonuser is at a disadvantage in expressing his own strongly held convictions because he must accept all other points of view as equally valid. Therefore, influence in process groups favors the user. As a practical outcome of youth culture, the power to command falls to the most reckless and entertaining among the students: the jokers and the users. And what defense does the facilitator have in the nondirective mode to keep this from happening? In the observations of Coulson, none.

The child "grows." And in the process, his defenses break down: He loses his fear of going against the prohibitions of home and church.

Coulson says if America goes under in the war on drugs, he'll say he's seen the educational form that shares the blame.

This education harms children because it centers authority in the child—in opposition to outside authority—and impedes learning. This approach fails to understand personhood.

The United States has a twenty year history of experimentation with person-centered education. During most of those years, scores on the Scholastic Aptitude Tests (SAT) for college application have dropped.

In a person-centered environment, test scores inevitably plummet because to oppose all authority is to oppose learning. Trust in and yielding to authority is the vehicle for receiving instruction. That's why novice therapists give themselves over to a master and copy him, even to the point of copying the sound of his voice. Under his influence they incorporate one manner after another. Then, through a kind of artistic integration, they find a voice of their own.

In spite of nondirective training, students of Carl Rogers valued his example and authoritative teaching. Consequently, some of them went through the artistic, imitative process. When a graduate heard two of them speak in the same cadence and inflection of their teacher, she was surprised. She knew that the person-centered approach emphasizes congruence—honesty in thinking, feeling, doing. "I could hardly tell them apart," she said. What happened to authenticity? she asked.

On the importance of authority outside of self, Michael Polanyi offers an illustration from the training of psychiatrists: A distinguished psychiatrist demonstrated to his students a patient who was having a mild fit of some kind. Later the class discussed the question whether this had been an epileptic or hysteroepileptic seizure. The matter was finally decided by the psychiatrist: "Gentlemen," he said, "you have seen a true epileptic seizure. I cannot tell you how to recognize it; you will learn this by more extensive experience." Until they could more fully understand what the psychiatrist based it on, students would learn to recognize seizures by accepting his diagnosis, Polanyi concluded.

Polanyi's point is that if everything must be spelled out, nothing taken on authority, then education stops at the point at which the professor knows more than he can tell. But if a student yields to that authority, he gains an indefinable learning he could not otherwise attain.[11]

Misunderstanding the function of authority arises from a basic misapprehension of the nature of personhood. Coulson explains it this way: After we strip the person of his culture in psychotherapy, we think we catch the *essence* of the person. But we're wrong. What we really catch is the *person in psychotherapy.*

Psychotherapy is one culture among many and is significant for what it leaves out. The client leaves behind his ordinary life skills—the skills that help him make a living, for example, and the skills that keep his life from flying apart. Why should we assume that the traits he develops in therapy will serve him better than those it took him years to develop in life? Don't forget that the therapist brings his skill to the clinical setting, but we don't look at him. We look at the client and say, "That's how everyone can be—like the client."

Are we going to discard all cultures other than the psychotherapeutic one? Are we going to prescribe only one model of the person? I would hate to think that person-centered therapy can explain the whole world. But that is exactly what the movement tries to do.[12]

For example, in the Immaculate Heart experiment, instead of enabling the nuns to fulfill their duties and their calling, the project team recast their identity. They interpreted "be true to yourself" as the necessity to break commitments and to cast off present obligations in favor of "*self*-fulfillment."[13] In essence they declared that there is no such thing as duty. What they didn't know was that keeping commitments and being a true self are part of the same package.

CSP leaders chased a rainbow, not reality. Not only a school system disintegrated but nuns and students told Coulson afterwards they regretted the pain and emptiness the new way brought. When belief in this uniform model becomes the standard by which to measure personality, high regard for the *therapeutic personality* eclipses appreciation for *the real person* under consideration. What a miscarriage of assessment.[14]

This education, a way of life, harms children because it springs from the seeds of a totalitarian mindset: Program promoters are neither responsive nor accountable. They sell totality and perfectionism, or utopianism. And in some cases, they force their way of life on the unwilling.

Taking each of the above three points, I state first that pushers—as opposed to followers—of this way of life are neither responsive nor responsible. They often exhibit a zeal that will not listen to opposition. Seemingly unaware of their own totalitarian bent, these activists become militant, if not abusive, against those who do not share their enthusiasm for a program. Then when the program fails, they blame causes outside the program. Most recently, the superintendent at Bainbridge Island blamed lack of community support.[15] Earlier, Carl Rogers blamed administrators, wealthy contributors who cut off support, and those "with strong religious commitment who hinder progress."[16]

Second, pushers of this education sell totality and perfectionism.[17] Psychologists thought their studies, based largely on the findings of therapy, reveal the human more fully. They got carried away with this vision and set out to sell it. No longer content to have devised successful methods for helping individuals one-to-one and in small groups, they embarked on a program of transforming the larger society.

From their viewpoint, relationships revealed in psychotherapy "seemed so pure," they thought principles should apply everywhere. Soon, however, when those methods proved inappropriate, even destructive, they could not easily bring themselves to back off; they became slaves to their own ideas.[18]

Third, too heavily invested by commitment, pushers of this education force their way of life on the unwilling.[19] This coercive feature of process education, however, violates what Carl Rogers taught: He advised that even advanced mental health professionals should not be *required* to take part in such education. He was adamant because research showed that such group work poses risks to participants and their families.[20]

"All would agree that [the intensive group experience] is potent," he said. He had observed a few psychotic episodes during or immediately after an intensive session. "It had some frightening moments," Rogers continued, "when its potency was very evident and I realized a particular person might be deeply hurt or greatly helped but I could not predict which."

"What was already clear was that, whether the experience was totally positive, totally negative or mixed, there were always risks in participation, and the risks were always personal," says Coulson. Therefore, Rogers believed group experience should never be forced upon anyone. And yet the schools, which minor children must attend according to law, fail to apply this same caution; they sometimes require group work without the knowledge or consent of parents.[21]

To ignore the facts of research and experience reveals the CSP team's unwillingness to be scientific in their discipline. They refused to listen to parents and veteran academicians who opposed them. They refused to recognize what works and what doesn't work. Even though the basic doctrine of this therapy is that no one knows what is best for someone else, the team thought they knew what was best for others. Therefore, they refused to give up the program. These signs reveal a totalitarian mindset.

Rogerian principles applied system-wide to school districts harm children because "school-based management," "site councils," "shared decision making,""trust agreements" increase likelihood for political maneuvering and make possible evasion of accountability to the public.

Although citizens ponder where lines of authority should lie, I've observed that successors of Carl Rogers do not ask which of the two shall be the authority—parents or the State. They shift attention to the *egalitarian* status of child, parents, and school authorities.[22] This attitude by educational power holders finds expression in radical change of structure for education. I've seen the person-centered egalitarianism of the classroom extended throughout a whole school district to include all personnel from custodians to administrators. And this extension *beyond* the classroom to management/employee relationships comes after twenty years of failure *within* the classroom!

In this restructuring at the beginning of 1990, public schools are following the Rogerian pattern. They are setting up "site councils," or school-based management, at schools that resemble the school-site schoolboards that Rogers proposed. Also new policy leaders favor "shared decision making" and "trust agreements" for "human interaction" between administration, classified personnel, unions, teachers, and students. These program backers now expect institutions to operate like encounter groups, with free expression of feelings, presided over by facilitators.[23] You know what happened to the Immaculate Heart College when it tried to implement these ideas system-wide!

This person-centered approach to school administration carries the potential for chaos. With everyone expressing feelings on an equal basis, no means exists to resolve real conflicts, short of one side saying, "My feelings are more important than yours."[24] That means that without an external standard or authority, politicking or intimidation wins, arbitrarily, without employing the logic of reason. Either that, or each matter must be arbitrated by a third legal party, which is not responsible to the electorate and which carries potential for politicization. Recently, it was disclosed that in the decentralized New York schools, more than a third of the school-based schoolboards have faced allegations of corruption and mismanagement.[25]

And there is yet another question more crucial than jurisdiction and "conflict resolution" here. (Conflict resolution is a major feature and topic of person-centered education.) That more important issue is responsibility.

In shifting responsibility in the egalitarian classroom or district, the child is the loser. A decision making classroom saddles him with more than immaturity can handle. And in the Rogerian restructured district, he loses in another way. In that framework, if he is victimized, his parents cannot locate an authority to petition because the Rogerian approach institutionalizes buck-passing. President Truman's quip, "the buck stops here," becomes "the buck never stops anywhere; it keeps going round and round"—from teacher to principal to union to superintendent to schoolboard to site council. And where it stops, nobody knows.

Granted, private enterprise is benefiting by making their structures less vertical and more horizontal in authority and responsibility. But owners still maintain final authority, and, more importantly, they spend their own money. In public school enterprise, however, the electorate needs closer check and balance control over those who spend money that is not their own. The problem with the educational power restructuring is its tendency toward power entrenchment through shared favor-trading and mutual cover-ups between administration and unions. But is it surprising that utopian-type philosophies spawn totalitarian-type structure?.

Now for a final word about this educational movement as summed up by Coulson: In the seventies and eighties, school authorities let a tidal wave of timidity about right and wrong wash over them. They allowed strange and reckless classroom exercises to take the place of confident instruction. It wasn't defensible then. In the nineties, it's criminal.[26]

6 WHAT EDUCATION WORKS?

WHAT EDUCATION WORKS AT HOME?

Coulson and his colleagues ran into it again and again in studying the offspring of families that pursue absorbing enterprise together. These children do not condemn their parents nor do they feel the need to forgive them. These children are grateful. By shared family enterprise, they receive experience beyond the skill or knowledge their parents impart.

Today with schools undermining family authority, family involvement is doubly important. Also, when education leads children into dangerous behavior, the family has to counteract that influence. Coulson suggests that you involve yourself with your child by teaching him what is dear to your own heart: athletics, music, art, carpentry, computers, books, stamp collecting—whatever *your* interest. Then when you release your child into adult life (or the influence of public schools), he has not only the interest or skill you pass along but also strength of character to meet whatever life offers.

Commitment together to a project, an interest, a group, a faith, an ideal is the glue that binds human beings together. "It is probably a sign of weakness not to want always to be free from commitment," writes Coulson. "I know that I am weak. Still, there is more to the idea of requirement than the simple rejection of freedom." There's also an unwillingness to be isolated. For to ask something of someone else, or to be asked, binds a person to the other.[1] Being part of something outside yourself gives you a sense of your own identity. Coulson agrees with that friend who wrote him a note, "A sign of my love for my friends is when I ask things of them." Maybe this is why children cry out for adults to set standards, to hold them to something higher than what they are able to reach in themselves, to give their lives shape and direction, to help them know who they are, to let them know they belong.

Of three keys, *the first key to successful family involvement is not force, but the parents' willingness to believe that they just might know better than their children what is good for them.*[2] *They have the courage and the cleverness to overcome their children's resistance to good training.*

Pop singer Bobby Vinton's parents figured out an unorthodox method to overcome Bobby's resistance to practice. They used bribery. "They paid me twenty-five cents an hour to practice the clarinet. . . My parents taught me persistence," Vinton said.[3] I include this example not as an ideal but to show that a plan of action may be in order.

"My father *pushed* me to the starting line," Nova Johnson said of her father Nunelly, who set an example. He was a screen writer, who kept regular office hours and often discussed his writing projects around the family hearth. Nova learned that you apply yourself diligently—none of this waiting around for a muse to inspire you. And even though her father is dead now, she still looks at her writing by his standards. "How he would like this, I think," she says about her work.[4]

Coach Tom Landry of the Dallas Cowboys football team knew the secret of successful involvement: "My job," he said, "is to get men to do what they don't want to do in order to achieve the goals they want to achieve."

The parents of Leslie Hodge knew this secret, too. Hodge began his career as a symphony conductor locked in the music room of his home.

"We lived in Albany, Australia," Hodge says. "I was seven years old. I was to practice the piano an hour a day, six days a week. My mother could tell when I was not in the mood. That's when she'd lock the door."

One day having developed a means of escape, Leslie climbed out the window. And along came his father, home early from work.

"Where do you think you're going, young man?"

"Into the music room, Father," said Leslie, thinking fast and reversing his direction.

"It isn't that my parents were severe," Hodge says. "I see them today as having done me a great favor. I wanted to play the piano—until it came time to practice. Then I wanted to avoid it. My parents didn't let me give in to temptation. They locked the door.

"I didn't take it lying down," he says. "I had so many tricks! I remember the day I learned I could open the front of the clock on the mantel in the music room, the clock that timed my practice sessions. I learned I could move the minute hand ahead.

"Father called on me at practice one Saturday afternoon. He looked at the clock. 'Leslie, there seems to be something wrong with that clock. It gains five minutes everyday except Sunday. You don't practice on

Sunday, do you?' He said no more. That was the end of the clock trick."

Through move and countermove, Leslie Hodge learned to play the piano. Once past his twelfth birthday—by then practicing was a firm habit—he knew he wanted to be a musician. Today, after years of performing and conducting around the world, he lives in La Jolla, helping youngsters learn to play.[5]

Papa Mozart was another father unafraid to exercise his paternal prerogatives. Without a society imposing upon him false guilt and as the preeminent music teacher of the age, Leopold could with confidence set aside other ambitions to foster his son's genius. Had he chosen otherwise, we would have no *Great Mass in C Minor*. For Leopold shared not only his music but also his faith with his son. "I have God always before my eyes. I recognize his power, I fear his anger; but I also know his love," Wolfgang wrote his father.

Hollywood condemns this father and psychologists warn about abuse of power, but Leopold had a different concern. "Genius threatens always to run off the page," he said. He was a teacher who had the self-discipline and patience to hold his pupil back in order to bring him along.

If a modern psychologist accused Leopold of training Wolfgang to satisfy his pride, Leopold would probably answer, "Of course, for my own sake I want to hear Wolfgang's song, but not for my benefit alone but for his blessing and for God's."

"After God, Papa" was the son's personal tribute to a father whom he revered.[6]

Awe of authority is common to the background of happy, productive adults. "They say Vince Lombardi was a great motivator. He couldn't teach my momma anything," says running back Earl Campbell of the Houston Oilers. Edwin Moses, Olympic hurdler and holder of a degree in physics, is another who held his parent in awe. "My father hated bad grades," he says. "I lived in fear of losing everything—athletics, social life, everything—if I got a C in school." So of course he toed the line.[7]

A second key to successful family involvement is that parents pass along to their children their own consuming passions. The lives of Bobby Vinton and Henry Mancini illustrate what I mean. Both of them had fathers who were frustrated amateur musicians. Vinton's father was a weekend orchestra leader in Canonsburg, Pennsylvania. Mancini's father played flute in the municipal band of Aliquippa. They got excited when their sons showed sparks of interest in music. They pushed; they lectured; they got involved.[8]

Sports-enthusiasts also often involve themselves with their children. Bob Feller and his father threw thousands of baseballs behind the barn in Iowa. After that Bob stepped right in as starting pitcher with Cleveland. This father made sure his son gained from his enthusiasm and expertise.

Because parents can cultivate the inborn ability and interest of the child, such strong parental interest needn't violate the child's own. Wonder boy jockey Steve Cauthen grew up sitting on bales of hay in the family barn, whipping them, practicing his technique. His father, a blacksmith, took his career in hand, putting him on a weight lifting program to increase strength, consulting with doctors about likely future growth, asking experienced riders to help him with his style. The child who fulfills the parents' longing can fulfill himself.

What goes for vocational direction goes for values, too; children need a focus when they are young. They need strong values if they are to prosper in a confusing world, but a parent can't teach what he doesn't believe in. He has no better values to give than his own—not necessarily the values he manages to live by. A parent who limits himself to teaching what he is able to practice might not have so much to teach. He must know that what he has to say is also important.[9]

This brings us to the third key to successful family involvement: Parents teach by precept. But because they listen to critics too much, they've laid aside this valuable tool. In the past, however, children credited parents by quoting them: "My father always said. . . "

"My mother *always* told me you can't do wrong and get away with it," Sharrieffa Barksdale answered when reporters asked why she hadn't used steroids. Sharrieffa believed her mother and stayed clean, but 1983 teammates at Pan American Games in Venezuela got caught cheating.

Mrs. Barksdale told her daughter, not once but many times—*always*—that "you can't do wrong and get away with it." Sharrieffa learned from someone other than herself. She didn't have to quote self-talk, "Myself, I've always said. . ." By the *otherness* and *obligatory character* of her parent's teaching, no less than its *constancy,* this winner could quote her wise mother.[10]

Michael Andretti also thanks a parent for *persistent* and *incessant lecturing.* "The one thing he emphasized over and over," reports Michael about his champion, Indianoplis, racecar-driving father, "was that I've got to respect the place. He *told me and told me* that when it catches up to you, it bites hard. . . He also *kept saying* that the time to be most careful is when the car isn't running quite right and you begin to think maybe it's your fault, and you start trying too hard. That's when he said the track will bite you for sure. There were times out there this month when, if my Dad hadn't *drummed it into me,* I would have done just that."

The mother of Isaac Isador Rabi, great Nobel Prize winner in physics, was more subtle but equally effective. "Did you ask any good questions today, Isaac?" she asked her son *everyday* after he got home from school.

How often should a parent repeat himself? Coulson's Law says, "The proper time to allot an important message is however long it takes to get it across."[11] He also gives parents permission to abandon the artificial ways of the clinical model and to take responsibility for what happens with their children. That's what the adults in the next two stories did. Their ways differ, but both got involved in creating good team members.

In 1989 Warriors basketball Coach Don Nelson did not try to hide his rancor when the subject came up about Lithuanian rookie Sarunas Marciulionis, one of the first few Eastern European bloc players in American professional basketball.

On January 7, 1990, Coach Nelson was not going to ease the pressure on him after just one night's outstanding game. "I've been hard on him lately because it's time now for him to start remembering some of the basic mistakes that he's making and to start eliminating those mistakes," Nelson said. "I'm not talking about the little things, but five basic, major things that we talk to him about *every single day, every game. . .*I'm going to make him or break him right now. In fact, after our game against Miami, we talked in my office for a long time, and it was hard on him in there. The next day, he had a great practice and he played the way we wanted him to play" (emphasis added). And Marciulionis kept playing through the season, newspapers show.[12]

As you read, contrast this success story with the next one. Also, remember that involvement means more than shared activity; it also means emotional investment. To abandon the psychotherapeutic model does not mean to abandon empathy. Coulson tells the doctor's true story in the first person:

Elizabeth was mad. Screaming about a papier-mache mask she need- ed for a first grade project, she stormed around the kitchen table. She wanted to form it by laying moistened paper towels over a balloon. Each time she smoothed on a new towel, the other wrinkled and slipped.

Mother was making dinner and couldn't help. Jane, our teenager, who sometimes can handle Elizabeth, had gotten mad herself and given up.

"Won't somebody help me? I can't do it. I'm not old enough—

AAUGH!" Another towel had slipped.

Eleven year old John spoke up. "Nobody wants to help you, Beth, because you holler at them."

For my part, I had retreated to the living room. But then I realized I faced a moment of decision. I could read the evening paper and shut out the noise. Parents of young children develop skill at shutting out noise. Or I could go back to the kitchen and shut up Elizabeth. I could throw the balloon and towels away and put Elizabeth in her room until she realized how to act like a decent person.

What to do with a little girl? How best to raise one? I get confused. But could I reverse the problem and find an answer? Could I ask what sort of person I wanted to be? I could. Then I knew I didn't want to be the avenger saying, "I'll teach you to cry!" And I knew I didn't want to be the coward, hiding in my paper. Instead, I remembered that I hadn't held my little girl on my lap in a long time, though I'd held my newspaper nightly.

I called Elizabeth into the living room and asked if she would sit on my lap. She did, and she cried and I felt good because I was holding a little human being in my arms. Soon she would be a big human being and it would be more awkward to hold her.

I asked John if he would come in. "John, you used to have a problem with crying, didn't you? I remember that the children used to tease you and call you a crybaby."

"Yes."

"But you stopped. Do you remember why?

"I was about six. I don't remember why I stopped. I know I got tired of the teasing. I guess I just grew up."

I didn't really think John could advise Elizabeth. She was in a phase. There were signs she was growing out of it already. But I had to note that by the time he and I had finished talking, Elizabeth had finished crying. That was good—a bonus. What was best, however, was that three people who didn't have to be, were in a room together. They lived together and often didn't notice. Now they were paying attention.

One of them, eleven years old, spoke softly of himself and of what it had been like to be six. One of them, just turned seven, lay in her daddy's arms. And one of them was pleased to be a father.[13]

The coach and the doctor took time *to get involved* with their charges. Finding time for his family was something Coulson used to ponder often as you can see from what he recorded years ago: "When I get busy, I miss my family. I don't mean I long for them because they are away. I mean I miss them even when they are right under my nose, for sometimes we just don't connect. Either I am busy or too tired to reach out or even to receive. Right now I am busy writing this. Afterward, I will be tired. My family will act satisfied if they share some of the same problems. Or they might wonder, 'Who is that man anyhow?'

"With strangers, it's different, sometimes more exciting. Should it be that way?"[14]

Other times Coulson did recognize opportunities to connect with his children. Years ago when they were young, they had basketball games in the backyard. And sometimes he'd join them, but he'd feel guilty. He'd think of the briefcase of work on his desk.

One day he tried to experiment with his mind. "What if your family were your work?" he asked himself. If that were the case, then he wouldn't feel guilty for playing basketball. He'd say he was studying the family.

Later he tried a long term plan to trick himself into spending time with his family. He formed a family jazz band. With this performing group, he could take everyone with him when he gave speeches.

After his family performed, in his talks he made a point I'd like to make now: Parents need to regain the confidence shattered by experts. For one thing parents are too critical of the quality of their family life. To illustrate how families should view their life together, he had each child in the band join the playing two bars after the other. No individual child sounded too good by himself, but by the time all of them played together, they sounded like real music makers.

"Music is more than the sum of the individual notes," he said, "and life is more than the sum of its isolated moments."[15]

Another example illustrates his point about appreciating the quality of family life over the long haul. The University of California Medical Center, San Francisco, studied fifty families by filming them at mealtime.

The scientists found little expression of joy by the families, not much intimacy or closeness. In only two of the families did the experimenters notice any touching. Most of the families talked a lot, but it wasn't happy talk. "Our happiest family," the chief scientist said, "was all deaf."

"I realized that if you looked at my own family as a series of isolated incidents," says Coulson, "it might not make good sense either. We have been known to fight. When the children were younger, it seemed hardly a meal went by but that some were calling others names. Freeze the frames of their interaction and look at them. It would look pretty bad. Yet even then I had the impression my family members would be caring for one another into the indefinite future.

"Life isn't like a stop-action movie. It's more like a jazz band. Joy isn't a single incident in our lives. Joy is having life together over time, looking back later and seeing that it was good, even if individual moments were bad."[16]

The Coulson Family Jazz Band was one family's answer to improve the current moments and to build up a treasury of family memories. The reason a family needs to rally around an activity is that the desire to meet and share thoughts and feelings for its own sake is not sufficient compulsion to make continued meeting likely. That's also the reason why the activity needs to be one that parents themselves appreciate.

And the enterprise is even better when it unites the family in some kind of real work enterprise. "In sharing responsibility for a work," Coulson writes, "family members become useful to one another." This gives young people a sense of importance, a sense of being needed— especially teenagers, who need something to do. "If the family doesn't find a respected place for its young people who will?" he asks.

In the early days of the Coulson Family Jazz Band, Coulson had written to the Sacramento Traditional Jazz Society, telling them his family would like to play at a monthly meeting. He told them they attended the previous Memorial Day festival and went home determined to play jazz.

Bill Borcher of the Jazz Society called and invited the Coulsons to the mid-winter festival to be one of nineteen West Coast bands.

The kids were flabbergasted. They hadn't expected a festival invitation. "How did they hear about us?"

"I told them," Coulson said.

"That worried my kids," says Coulson. "They say I'm prone to exaggeration. They say they don't recognize themselves in some of the stories I tell about them. "If they're going on what you said about us, Dad, they're going to have pretty high expectations."

"Then we'll have to live up to them," Coulson said.

One of those frantic months followed that have turned out to be so good for the Coulsons' learning. At times they got on one another's nerves, but by the end of the month they were eighty percent ready. The rest came in the car on the way and in the hotel room closet once they'd arrived.[17]

When the children were growing up, the Coulson Family Jazz Band worked. It made them get to know each other and love each other more. The other examples I gave worked, too.

Educational experts, listen! Don't throw out the ageless principles of teaching. In a changing world, anchors are even more important.

If it works, don't fix it!

WHAT EDUCATION WORKS AT SCHOOL?

What works at school? Instruction about objective material with standards that stretch children in their abilities and in their vision, I'd say.

And beyond that if moral questions are to be raised at school about sexual activity and drug use, then the truth also needs to be told in these life and death matters. Rogers lost some of his following when he wrote about marriage *and its alternatives.* In my opinion, the schools lose their following when they talk about abstinence *and its alternatives.* In this day of AIDS and a drug epidemic, we don't need to talk about alternatives. Even the law agrees that minor children should abstain.

Parents can deal with society's influence. They can turn the knob on the television. They can oversee the activities and associations of their children. But they can't fight the influence of the school that says sexual activity and drug use are a matter of choice. School and teacher influence are too powerful and too pervasive in our society. Even for children kept out of these decision making programs, the educational environment of the public schools affects all children in the community—even those in private schools.

From his own experience, Coulson tells about an example of the kind of drug and sex education that lays out the truth in clear terms. He belongs to a group that originated Neversmoke. In marijuana country in the Emerald Triangle in Mendocino County, California, he worked as a Neversmoke volunteer. These men teach about smoking and carry over the application to other dangerous substances, too.

The program includes excerpts from a film *Death in the West*, the true story of the Marlboro cowboy; also, x-ray illustrations of cancer growth in the lungs of a smoker. A jazz group provides free-wheeling counterpoint to the serious campaign. Repertoire includes smoker Louis Armstrong's "Someday You'll be Sorry" (Jazz history's greatest innovator died of heart disease); also smoker Duke Ellington's "Don't Get Around Much Any More (Lung cancer killed him); smoker Billie Holiday's version of "All of Me" (Drugs took all of her in the prime of life).

Neversmoke exposes the cigarette marketing strategy behind decision making programs. Then students see why cigarette companies want parents to look the other way while children "decide." Students also see that if parents actively teach their children about the dangers of smoking and about heart and lung health, children will abstain and cigarette companies will go out of business—because almost no one takes up smoking in adulthood any more.

An important part of Neversmoke is to teach students to analyze cigarette advertising. In surveying advertisements, children see that the tobacco industry is not timid about giving out imperatives. They look at "Light my Lucky" and "Come to Marlboro Country" ads and note the emotional appeal. [18]

A powerful tool in Neversmoke—even though dealing with children—is to appeal to the noble instincts of parenthood.[17] The *Neversmoke* approach doesn't underestimate the capacity of students to look beyond present "need fulfillment" to rise to the higher perspective of thinking about a future family.   Students determine that they will need to give their children a counter-force to prepare them to withstand advertising hype. And by looking ahead, they can see more clearly what they want for themselves.

Neversmoke also addresses the subject of what the group calls Sexexcess. In so doing, they keep the same focus as in the subject of smoking—that is, to help students realize their hopes for a better life for their own children.

Students learn that society gives them wrong messages that they don't have to buy into. They learn that abstinence from sexual intercourse before marriage is desirable, normal, and possible. The present message they receive is that society expects young people to be sexually active and that young abstainers must suffer the pain of being, at best, classified immature, or, horror of horrors, different from everyone else.

Remember, Doc tells students, as a parent you are an author, too. You are the text your children will edit; they'll pass that text along to the next generation of editors. And educators, too, author young lives in their care. That's continuity.

We're writing the script, Doc Nevermore concludes. What will it be?[19]

7 TIMELESS PRINCIPLES FOR GOOD EDUCATION

and AUTHOR'S CALL FOR ACTION

To get to a jungle site, a father carries a little one, who cannot walk the distance. An observer can tell that the scantily clad tribesman-father loves his little son. Although the two belong to the twentieth century, their life in the jungle resembles that of their ancient forbears.

In this National Geographic film, Father takes four year old son Ali in his arms to show him what an edible ant looks like—for he doesn't want to expose his young child to the danger of eating inedible ants. Life in the jungle requires that the father warn his son of minute variations in the ant family. With tenderness Father holds Ali and quietly shows him these things not because he wants to abuse the power that he has over him and not because of selfish desire to control but because he loves his son.[1]

Zeroing in on the jungle scene helps me highlight for further consideration those principles of education that are timeless. This examination will anchor us in educational principles that help children. If we arm ourselves with the facts about what's good, we can recognize that which is harmful. Let's take the principles one by one.

First, *Father carries Ali to the faraway instruction site. And because there are real dangers in the world, Father warns Ali about them.*

Today we force children to carry themselves through drug war zones and sex traps. In essence, we refuse to name what's edible and what is not. The child has to decide for himself. Unlike Ali's father, we shove our children out into known dangers in life and imagine we have done a good thing.

Second, *Father in gentleness and love expresses nobility of character.*

Since psychologists tend to interpret all behavior as self-serving, how can they understand the parental role? If they rule out the possibility of self-sacrifice or nobility of character, how can they recognize mother love for what it is? How can they acknowledge the cohesion of character fatherhood often inspires?

Carl Rogers says that for the man of tomorrow relationships are not meant to be permanent but fluid. In this framework, family members are no longer so significant. Mother can talk only about her feelings and Junior only about his. And so each one ends up talking about himself all the time. And neither feels a sense of obligation toward the other.[2]

When in this way counselors and educators explain behavior solely in self-serving terms, they drag us all down. For once we see whatever we do as self-serving, our behavior is on its way to becoming random; then one choice will be as good or as bad as another. And, may I add, how good can educators be who disdain even aspiration for goodness?

When we accept the psychologists' assessment of our motives, we parents become introspective and confused. For to examine what we respect in such a detached manner, Michael Polanyi writes, is to destroy its uplifting power. "Then law is no more than what the courts will decide," he writes, "morality but a convention, tradition but an inertia, God but a psychological necessity. Then man dominates a world in which he himself does not exist. . . He has lost his voice and his hope and has been left behind meaningless to himself."

But regardless of what authorities claim, we parents incline toward making moral judgments on our children's behalf. And with that moral perspective we seek to live out before our children the standard we uphold. That's what prompts us and them to higher levels of living.[3]

Third, *Ali cannot find the truth for himself; he needs a teacher.* Ali cannot look within himself to discern the difference between two ants. He cannot talk it over with his peers to find the answer. He cannot make his own valid decision, which no on else has the right to question. He does not know the right ant from the wrong ant. He doesn't know what's dangerous and what's safe.

Fourth, *Father teaches Ali about others.* Ali can't hold himself. Father has to offer those strong, protective arms to him. Ali is a child. He's dependent for his welfare upon his father's care and instruction. Father teaches him, not the self-centeredness of psychotherapy but the attraction and commitment of "otherness," which is the basis of love.[4]

In 1977 at the University of California, La Jolla, an encounter group learned about otherness. There a wise word jolted a group to its senses, at least momentarily. An angry participant felt that the group had been judging him, treating him not like an angry person but like *an angry person case.* When he lashed out, accused parties felt bad. A discussion ensued. Shouldn't they have done this? Done that? Yes, but. . . No one denied the angry one the right to express himself because that was inviolable. On that point all humanistic theories agree.

So no one questioned the participant's right to complain—except a foreigner, Miko. "You have the freedom—I do—to express anger. But sometime to do so hurt person. I don't want to hurt person."

Her word was the last, because what she said was so simple, so right. Call it a reminder of what manners must once have been. Or call it poetry. Miko knew what "otherness" is about.[5]

Fifth, *Father accepts his responsibility, and Ali responds to his authority.* This is how learning takes place. Ali accepts the fact that his father knows best; he does his part, pays attention, listens, and survives. And Father does not betray that trust.

"All practical learning is based on authority," Michael Polanyi wrote. The learner, he said, has only to submit to the authority of the instructor, who has the knowledge and skill he needs. To do this, the student must be confident his master understands what he is trying to teach him and that he, the student, will eventually succeed in his turn in understanding the meaning of the things that are being explained to him.[6]

A young friend told Coulson about a class in x-ray reading. The first times the instructor pointed out signs on the x-ray, students thought he was imagining things. They could see shadows of the ribs and heart and a few blotches in between and no lungs at all. Over time, however, as the instructor kept talking and pointing, the students began to see. Through the instructor's persistence, what didn't exist before began to emerge.

What if the x-ray instructor followed modern advice for teaching? He would have to listen, then say, "Maybe you're right. Maybe what I see isn't there." But from experience the instructor knows better and he can't say that. Apply that analogy to teacher and child. Teachers know more than children, and they are responsible for what they know.[7]

Participants in affective education of the now-defunct Immaculate Heart College told Coulson they felt betrayed by the CSP team. Participants did their part; they submitted to the team's authority, but the team did not carry through with its part, responsibility. For whether they accepted or disavowed their mantle of authority, they were responsible for beginning that "pattern of failure."[8]

Sixth, *Father knows the content of his message is important. He does not teach Ali a process only.* With confidence and seriousness this teacher imparts to this student information. What more need I say?

Seventh, *Father is directive, not nondirective; he is not afraid to lecture Ali as he shows him the ant.*

Can I deny that there are always nonconformists in any group who will interpret instruction or advice as a challenge to do the opposite? No, I can't. But it's time we stop gearing our whole system toward those few and start paying attention when a lot of children suffer from our choices.

Furthermore, even rebels don't benefit from touchy-feely exercises. In reality, the red flags they throw out signal to mature adults the need for them to take these children in hand and point them in the right direction. Inmates often attest to this truth. The superintendent of a center for delinquent boys in New Jersey quotes a seventeen year old inmate: "When I grow up and have kids of my own, I would teach them the right way before they got too old. . . I got away with a lot of things."[9]

Eighth, *Father does not try to separate Ali from his family or his culture. He seeks to integrate him into his own time and place.* Father teaches Ali the ways of the jungle that his own family and culture have taught him. He does not disregard the trails already blazed.

This kind of trusting involvement begins with each new life. The infant learns his new culture when he utters his first baby babbling. That's how he learns language. He trusts those around him enough to imitate them and to try to communicate with them. He doesn't make the rules; he follows them. And the child's parent does not impede his language learning by making him wait until he can decide for himself which language to learn. If he did, the child might never communicate or have a mind. And no more than for language does a child choose his culture. It's impossible to be born without entering a particular culture.[10]

Coulson recommends that educators not alienate students from family and society but instead draw these children further into their culture. He considers mutual responsibility a defining characteristic of humankind and that cultural and human growth are imperiled to the extent that generations draw away from one another and from the world.[11]

Ninth, *Father tells Ali the truth about his world. He does not discount what he knows simply because of the boundaries of his experience.*

Not everyone can know everything; therefore, a scientist must rely upon the knowledge of fellow scientists, said Michael Polanyi. So too does Father depend on others; he draws upon his heritage. Trusting in the authority of others, each rises above personal limitations.

But if a person believes what he does by accident of birth, then can we not question the validity of those beliefs? Father sees the world differently from an American. Does not this observation dictate that truth must be subjective and relative, not objective and absolute? At first Maslow said yes. Later, however, he concluded that truth transcends culture.

"In recent years, and to this day," Maslow wrote, "most humanistic scholars and most artists have shared in the general collapse of all traditional values. And when these values collapsed, there were no others readily available as replacements. And so today, a very large proportion of our artists, novelists, dramatists, critics, literary and historical scholars are disheartened or pessimistic or despairing, and a fair proportion are nihilistic or cynical. [They believe] that no 'good life' is possible and that the so-called higher values are all a fake and a swindle.

"[We are in] a chaos of relativism. No one of these people now knows how and what to choose, nor does he know how to defend and to validate his choice. This chaos may fairly be called valuelessness."

Though an avowed atheist, Maslow did not deny truth and absolutes.

Tenth, *Father knows his calling. He knows who he is and what he is to do in his life.* He doesn't have to search his soul or discard his parents' way of life to find his identity. He can see and accept the obligations into which he is born. How foolish for him or for us to abandon what culture accumulates for our benefit! Instead of asking parents to bow out, Coulson recommends that they set up for their children cultural apprenticeship.[12]

After Coulson's involvement in this educational movement, Michael Polanyi is the one who helped him see more clearly. Whereas others had tried to influence Coulson and whereas he himself knew something was wrong, Polanyi provided the missing intellectual link he needed.

Instead of advocating escape from life by doing your own thing, Polanyi spoke of "calling." He said that just as none of us can escape our body but must relate to the world through equipment we receive, so too we cannot escape the particularity of our cultural upbringing, the basis of our one and only life cycle. In Polanyi's words, "I am called upon . . . to acquire the instruments of intelligence from my earliest surroundings," to use them "to fulfil the universal obligation to which I am subject."[13]

Maslow also in the 1950s expressed his belief in a commitment to a calling. One day to a roomful of future psychologists, he described self-actualizing people as those committed to a cause or mission in life. Then he asked, "How many of you plan to become *great* psychologists—another Freud?" No hands went up. "Why not?" he demanded. "Who will be the great leaders in psychology if not you?"

Eleventh, *Father accepts the obligations of his calling—in his case, survival in the jungle.* What relief Coulson felt in Polanyi's teaching! In school he had accepted his obligations. And now from Polanyi, he was learning that he still has obligations. When he accepted "the tasks that life set him"—in philosopher Viktor Frankl's terms—he found what he needed, his place in the world, a sense of belonging. We can learn from others and other cultures without divorcing our own past, he learned.[14]

Twelfth, *Father accepts his commitment to normal human ties—in this case responsibility for the survival of his son.* "The postman drops a letter in my mailbox as I sit down to write," Coulson wrote in 1979. "The letter announces a lot of changes in the life of a participant in a recent humanistic workshop. I know what is coming: There has been another divorce. Members of our team seem to have learned what conditions to provide to strengthen individuals—at the expense of their commitments." Is this a forward or a backward move?

Thirteenth, *Father knows the boundaries of the world he inhabits. Therefore, he does not fall into the trap of perfectionism or overextension of his philosophical insights.*

Self-determination within a culture has intrinsic limits of thought patterns, Coulson states. These are not absolute limits, else there would be no possibility of progress. But there is no unlimited, culture-free view of the world as Rogers projected—neither the therapist's nor the Pope's.

In *Tacit Dimension,* Polanyi wrote, "Whether his calling lies in literature or art, or in moral and social reform, even the most revolutionary mind must choose as his calling a small area of responsibility, for the transformation of which he will rely on the surrounding world as its premises."

Polanyi points out the danger of thinking that a person or a way can transform everything for everybody. "Perfectionism," he writes, "which would transform the whole of thought and the entire society, is a program of destruction, ending at best in a world of pretense."[15]

That's what the psychologists had tried to do. They wanted to do away with tradition and convert the world, and when the world did not respond, they became totalitarian in their ways. Coulson wrote of this, not to condemn, but as an insider looking back at early experimentation.

The therapeutic view sees the teaching of parental and traditional values as a barrier to personal development in children. Coulson believes, however, that if this humanistic view becomes the norm, it will actually *arrest* the further development of what is specifically human.[16]

That raises a question I'd like to answer: What is the most distinctive endowment of mature humanity? Don't human beings differ from animals and computers? Animals can think and feel. And rats in mazes and computers can even choose value by the decision making formula— that is, by making decisions according to alternatives and consequences. But man has a higher calling, higher than thinking, feeling, or deciding. Only he can make moral choices on the basis of truth. Only he can cherish convictions of truth, some for which he might be willing to die.

Computers do not have that capacity, but they can replicate and caricature the active listening of a therapist. According to Arno Penzias, Joseph Weizenbaum accomplished that in the field of artificial intelligence with his pioneering program ELIZA. He did this by creating a series of response recipes that could substitute for the patterned responses of a therapist.

For example, Weizenbaum predicted that a sentence fragment of the form "everybody. . . me" would reflect a recent experience. So, the statement, "Everybody makes fun of me," might elicit from ELIZA, "Tell me who made fun of you in the last few days." When asked a question with a noun in it, ELIZA might answer, "Why are you interested in" followed by the noun repeated and a question mark. Like a nondirective therapist, ELIZA could respond by inverting statements or asking for more information about one of the nouns in a sentence. The program also interspersed stock phrases like "Please go on."

Here is how a sample conversation might go:

Questioner: Are you really a psychiatrist?

ELIZA: Why are you interested in a psychiatrist?

Questioner: I'm not really interested in a psychiatrist.

ELIZA: You say that you are not really interested in a psychiatrist.

Questioner: That's right. I never had hang-ups about parents or stuff like that.

ELIZA: Tell me some more about your parents.

ELIZA fooled some people, who refused to believe that they had been conversing with a machine and not with a person giving the typed feedback. And even though a computer lacks empathy, which is supposed to accompany nondirective education, some participants later protested losing their regular sessions with "the friendly therapist." [17]

Coulson says that he appreciates nondirective, active listening in therapy and as an occasional tool elsewhere. But at the point at which it stops being only a technique and becomes a way of centering on personhood for a total philosophy for life, it falls short. I, too, think the approach does not represent man in his highest expression.

In conclusion, I consider dangerous any program of education that teaches—whether directly or indirectly—that truth and absolutes do not exist. Not only does such a philosophy undercut what being human is all about and not only does it lead children into dangerous behavior, but it violates the rights and authority of parents in relation to minor children.

AUTHOR'S CALL FOR ACTION

What can you do about this education that harms children?

Stand up and shout! Jump up and down!

And for whatever else the job takes, you must be willing.

Decision making programs are easy to spot but difficult to confront because the educational hierarchy can keep the target moving. One way is to shift the emphasis from an objectionable feature of a program to a seemingly attractive one. Another way—if a program falls into disfavor—is to repackage it under a new name. If that will not suffice, new terminology will throw observers off. With the program thus switching mix or match outfits, presenting a different face, and speaking a new language, who will recognize the impostor? Only the alert.

One tactic administrators and boards use to win acceptance for the scope and sequence is to say that it is only the "what" and not the "how." They say that implementation comes later and that later is the time to talk about what kind of program(s) to choose. That response is supposed to fend off objections as irrational. This is a tactic to forestall opposition so that the decision making program can get an *official* foothold *throughout* the system; in most cases, it already operates unofficially in isolated classrooms. Don't be misled. Be assured that the reason topics typical of these programs are segregated from the academic curriculum into a new one is in order to establish and entrench affective education.

You can recognize this education that harms when you see grouped into a separate curriculum topics like personal identity, death and dying, depression, suicide, relaxation techniques, stress management, self-esteem, addiction, and sex education. Without a doubt such a scope and sequence is the framework for a decision making program.

Sometimes innocent parties who are not agenda conscious may introduce a harmful program. If that is the case, they will be reasonable;

they will pay attention to documented research, listen to convincing evidence, care about the feelings of parents, and abandon the project.

But if an agenda is being pushed, promoters keep pushing in spite of public outcry. They do this in the face of solid research evidence showing that the proposed curriculum has proved harmful. And they possess no evidence to the contrary. Fueled by emotional enthusiasm alone, all they can offer is *subjective* appraisal

Also, if an agenda is being pushed, the establishment is not likely to discard the program no matter how strong nor how reasonable the resistance. If the public resists, however, the administration may modify a program to make it more acceptable. This can bring secondary improvements. Unfortunately, however, even though such changes do not alter the nature of the program, they will probably hide from an uninformed public the program's harmfulness.

If in spite of everything, the scope and sequence of the curriculum is adopted, then you can do four things: One, involve yourself in your child's life and ground him in your teachings. Two, if you can't take a child out of the school, take him out of those programs (see form in appendix). Three, monitor and resist. To cope with harmful instruction given without your knowledge or consent, teach your child what to watch for, to alert you and to protect himself. Four, choose alert, conscientious schoolboard members.

You resist because you're working for the good of the child, sound principles and practices, excellence in education, the rights of parents and citizens, and free access to information (often sorely lacking where these programs exist). But be forewarned: If you don't put your whole heart and head into this effort, you'll lose this fierce and longterm battle; it's not for cowards. You'll have to overcome intimidation and outlast the pushers.

Even though it may not seem so at first, remember you have the public on your side. One or two may have to work alone until others gain hope and courage. In the end, however, you'll find that parents of all backgrounds and beliefs care about the good of their children and will join you.

Be informed.

Inform others.

Then be willing to resist and persist.

The ways and means I leave to your imaginative resourcefulness.

Form for California residents. Others, omit references to law.

EXCUSE OF PUPIL FROM OBJECTIONABLE EDUCATION

TO: President and Members of the Schoolboard, Superintendent, Principal, Teachers:

I am the parent or guardian of _____, who is

enrolled in the _____ grade at _____ school of the

_____ school district.

This letter is written, legal notice that I am exercising my rights under California law (Education Code Sections 51240, 51550, and 51820) to request that the above-named pupil be excused from and not attend or participate in any class, presentation, project, extracurricular activity, or program presented by the school district or by agents under its direction, which involve any of the following:

sex or family life education; the acquiring or use of birth control drugs or devices; killing of prenatal babies by abortion; infanticide; euthanasia or suicide; homosexuality; bestiality, sadism, masochism, or other sexual perversions; showing of an R or X rated (pornographic) films; "values clarification"; or the use of questionnaires, role playing, or other strategies to question, expose or criticize any private, religious or moral values of the above-named pupil or members of his/her family

This notice applies not only to direct sex or family life education programs, but also to any of the abovementioned subjects which may be infused or included as "part of any course which pupils are required to attend" (as provided in Education Code Section 51550).

I expect to be notified of the presentation of materials and subjects as required by Education Code Section 48980 and of the approximate date of their presentation as required by Education Code Section 48983, so that I may exercise my right to inspect and review instructional plans and materials, as provided in Education Code Sections 51550 and 51820; and in order that I may monitor the exemption of the above-named pupil from classes or activities involving the above-mentioned objectionable subjects.

I request that the principal and all teachers or other agents of the school district who are involved with the education of the above-named pupil be informed of this legal, written notice, and that they be aware of the penalty of revocation or suspension of certification document for knowingly violating my rights, as provided for in Education Code Section 51550.

I request written acknowledgment of receipt and filing of this written, legal notice.

Signed: _____   Dated: _____

Address: _____

_____

Telephone number: (____) _____

SOURCE NOTES

Reference refers to previous paragraph unless otherwise indicated.

Chapter 1: WHAT IS THIS EDUCATION THAT HARMS?

1. Four paragraphs: Coulson, W. R. 1980. From client-centered therapy to the person-centered approach and back again. *Panel Discussion at the University of San Diego* (August 2). San Diego.

2. Coulson, W. R. 1987. Principled morality vs. consequentialism. *Research Council on Ethnopsychology*. San Diego, as summarized in the unpublished ACS report (footnote 8): page 6.

3. Coulson, W. R.1981. Lecture Notes. *USIU Psychology 640: Life-Cycle Human Development* (Fall): page 6. San Diego.

4. Coulson, W. R. I'm no masterpiece. Magnificat. *Center for Enterprising Families*. La Jolla. CA

5. Chandler, Russell. 1988. New Age epidemic in Christian Reader from *Understanding the New Age*. Irving, TX.

6. Coulson, W. R. 1989. The Seventh Sense: Case studies of parents protecting their children. *Center for Enterprising Families*. La Jolla, CA.

7. Coulson, W. R. 1987. Does therapy belong in the classroom?: page 2. *Education Reporter* (November): Number 22.

8. Coulson, W. R. I'm no masterpiece. *Magnificat. Center for Enterprising Families*. La Jolla, CA.

9. Idea of Coulson, W. R. 1987. Principled morality vs. consequentialism. *Research Council on Ethnopsychology*. San Diego.

10. One program is STAGES based on Elisabeth Kubler-Ross's stages of dying.

11. For example, Beyond War sponsored an art contest for elementary children. Also, The Aesthetic Approach sponsored Earth Day Art Festival.

12. For example, on a trip to study coastal Indians, children composed an Indian prayer and re-enacted it.

13. A local superintendent and schoolboard officially co-sponsored with Beyond War a workshop for teachers, encouraging them to adopt a "spiritual" worldview of the earth, a "new cosmology," a New Age philosophy.

14. Gordon, Thomas. 1974. *T.E.T. Teacher Effectiveness Training*. New York.

15. Coulson, W. R. 1989. Video tape. Southeastern Christian Church. Louisville, KY.

16. Quotation from student text examined by Coulson: *Health Education: The Search for Values*. (Read, Donald, Sidney Simon, Joel Goodman. 1977. New York.) See Coulson, W. R. 1987. Chick Koop's breakthrough: page 8. *Nevermore Associates*. La Jolla, CA.

17. Two paragraphs: Coulson, W. R. 1987. Chick Koop's breakthrough. *Nevermore Associates*. La Jolla, CA.

18. Four paragraphs: Coulson, W. R. 1988. On being lobbied. Memo to *Federal Drug Education Curricula Panel* (April 23).

19. Three paragraphs: Coulson, W. R. 1987. Principled morality vs.

consequentialism. *Research Council on Ethnopsychology.* San Diego.
20. Re speech by Rogers: Coulson, W. R. 1987. The Californication of Carl Rogers. *Fidelity* (November): 20 - 29.
21. Three and a half paragraphs. Coulson, W. R. 1987. Abstinence best Aids defense. *San Diego Union* (July 23): Commentary B-11. Also, Confessions of an ex-sexologist. 1988. *Social Justice Review* (March/April): 43 - 47.
22. Coulson, W. R. 1987. Chick Koop's breakthrough: page 1. *Nevermore Associates.* La Jolla, CA.
23. Sentence idea: Coulson, W. R. 1989. Video: Education that harms. Southeast Christian Church. Louisville, KY.
24. Coulson, W. R. and Carl Rogers.1968. From the manuscript of Second edition of *On Having No Choice:* pp. 2, 3. Columbus, OH
25. Coulson, W. R. 1987. Principled morality vs. consequentialism: page 5 and footnote 14. *Research Council on Ethnopsychology.* San Diego.
26. Sentence: Ibid: page 4.

Chapter 2: THE FAILED TEST OF EXPERIENCE

1. Coulson, W. R. "Daddy Maslow" from Coulson, W. R. 1989. Video: Education that harms. Southeast Christian Church. Louisville, KY.
2. Coulson, W. R. 1988. Focus: Classroom courses promote drugs and sex. *Education Reporter* (June): 3.
3. Coulson, W. R. 1988. On being lobbied. Memo to *Federal Drug Education Curricula Panel* (April 23).
4. Hoffman, Edward. 1988. *The Right to Be Human:* Page 113. Jeremy Tarcher. Los Angeles.
5. Two paragraphs: Hoffman, Edward. 1988. *The Right to Be Human:* Page 245. Jeremy Tarcher. Los Angeles.
6. Ibid.: Page 266.
7. Maslow, Abraham. 1979. *The Journals of A. H. Maslow. Vols. 1 and 2.* Brooks/Cole. Monterey, CA.
8. Ibid.
9. Maslow, Abraham. 1965. The taboo of tenderness, a lecture at Brandeis University.
10. Coulson, W. R. and Carl Rogers.1968. From the manuscript of Second edition of *On Having No Choice:* page 7. Columbus, OH.
11. Coulson, W. R. 1988. On being lobbied: page 7. Memo to *Federal Drug Education Curricula Panel* (April 23).
12. Coulson, W. R. and Carl Rogers. 1968. From the manuscript of Second edition of *On Having No Choice:* page 7. Columbus, OH.
13. Council on Smoking and Stupidity. 1987. Cigarettes and the self-esteem scam. *Center for Enterprising Families.* Comptche, CA.
14. Maslow, Abraham. 1979. *The Journals of A. H. Maslow. Vols. 1 and 2.* Brooks/Cole. Monterey, CA.
15. Coulson, W. R. Videotape: Saturday A.M. Southeast Christian Church.

Louisville, KY.

16. Coulson, W. R. and Carl Rogers. 1968. From the manuscript of Second edition of *On Having No Choice:* . Columbus, OH.

17. Maslow, Abraham. 1979. *The Journals of A. H. Maslow. Vols. 1 and 2.* Brooks/Cole. Monterey, California.

18. Coulson, Maslow. 1988. On being lobbied: page 4. Memo to *Federal Drug Education Curricula Panel* (April 23).

19. Hoffman, Edward. 1988. *The Right to Be Human.* Jeremy Tarcher. Los Angeles.

20. Maslow, Abraham. 1979. Humanistic Education vs. Professional Education: Further Reflections. *Journal of Humanistic Psychology* (Summer).

21. Maslow, Abraham. Revised ed. 1970. *Motivation and Personality.* NY.

22. Coulson, Maslow. 1988. On being lobbied: page 4. Memo to *Federal Drug Education Curricula Panel* (April 23).

23. Hoffman, Edward. 1988. *The Right to Be Human:* page 298. Jeremy Tarcher. Los Angeles.

24. Coulson, Maslow. 1989. To Johnson, Mark L., M. D. *Research Council on Ethnopsychology* (June 17). La Jolla, CA.

25. Coulson, W. R. 1988. To Wolpert, John: page 1. *United States International University* (May 12). San Diego.

26. Coulson, Maslow. 1988. On being lobbied: page 2. Memo to *Federal Drug Education Curricula Panel* (April 23).

27. Ibid.: page 3

28. Council on Smoking and Stupidity. 1987. Cigarettes and the self-esteem scam: page 1. *Center for Enterprising Families.* Comptche, CA.

29. Coulson, W. R. Videotape: Education that harms. Southeast Christian Church. Louisville, KY.

30. Four paragraphs: Coulson, W. R. A synthesis.

31. Coulson, W. R. 1987. Does therapy belong in the classroom? *Education Reporter:* (November). Number 22: page 2.

32. Coulson, W. R. About 1984. Backlash against the person-centered approach: page 25. For the *German Client-centered Therapy Association.*

33. Coulson, W. R. About 1984. Backlash against the person-centered approach: pp. 24, 25. For the *German Client-centered Therapy Association.*

34. Ibid.: page 23.

35. Sentence. Coulson, W. R. Tearing down the temple: Confessions of a Catholic school dismantler: page 18. *Fidelity:* (December): page 18.

36. Coulson, W. R. About 1984. Backlash against the person-centered approach: page 24. For the *German Client-centered Therapy Association.*

37. Ibid.: page 27.

38. Two paragraphs: Ibid.: page 22.

39. Four paragraphs. Coulson, W. R. 1979. *The Strength Test:* page 4. Helicon House. La Jolla, CA.

Chapter 3: THE FAILED TEST OF RESEARCH

1. Sentence. Coulson, W. R. Principled morality vs. consequentialism: page 3, footnote 8 re quote of Rick Little. *Research Council on Ethnopsychology.* San Diego.
2. Three paragraphs. Ibid.: page 6
3. Four paragraphs: Coulson, W. R. Principled morality vs. consequentialism: page 3. *Research Council on Ethnopsychology.* San Diego. Also, 1987. Chick Koop's breakthrough: page 7. *Nevermore Associates.* La Jolla, CA. And 1988. On being lobbied: page 9. Memo to *Federal Drug Education Curricula Panel* (April 23).
4. Six paragraphs: 1985. Re Helping Youth Decide: Fox/geese: page 2. *New York State Journal of Medicine:* Vol. 85 (July).
   Reports: Brook, Whiteman , Gordon, Brook. 1983. Fathers and sons: their relationship and personality characteristics associated with the son's smoking behavior. *J Genetic Psychol*; 142: 271 - 281.
   Wilson, Wood, Sicurella. 1982. Randomized clinical trial of supportive followup for cigarette smokers in a family practice. *Can Med Assoc J*; 126: 127 - 129.
5 . Six paragraphs: Pereira, Joseph. 1989. Alarming result: Even a school that is leading the drug war grades itself a failure: Students say why Bainbridge, after a 12-year effort, hasn't stemmed abuse. Struggling to interest parents. Wall Street Journal: Vol. CXXI No. 93 (November 10).
6. See last section of this chapter under second question.
7. Five paragraphs: Coulson, W. R. 1989. Sex education research: To concerned parent. *Director, Graduate Program in General Psychology, United States International University* (February 6). San Diego. Also, videotape: Education that harms. Southeast Christian Church. Louisville, KY.
   Quotes from Marsiglio, William and Frank Mott. 1986. The impact of sex education on sexual activity, contraceptive use and premarital pregnancy among American teen-agers. *Family Planning Perspectives:* pp. 151-162 (July/August).
8. Five paragraphs: Coulson, W. R. 1987. Principled morality vs. consequentialism: page 5. *Research Council on Ethnopsychology.* San Diego.
9. Two paragraphs: Coulson, W. R. About 1984. Backlash against the person-centered approach: pp. 10, 13. For the *German Client-centered Therapy Association.*
10. Coulson, W. R. About 1984. Backlash against the person-centered approach: page 11. For the *German Client-centered Therapy Association.* Quote from *Polanyi & Prosch.* 1975: page 203.
11. Three paragraphs. Coulson, W. R. 1988. On being lobbied: pp. 10, 11. Memo to *Federal Drug Education Curricula Panel* (April 23).
12. Six paragraphs. Coulson, W. R. 1989. Concerning Quest. To Mrs. Terry

Fennig. *Research Council on Ethnopsychology* (February 15). San Diego.

13. Doctoral candidate, international. Re drug education (in his son's public school). *United States International University (USIU)*. San Diego.

14. Coulson, W. R. Audio tape. Iowa WHO radio talkshow.

Chapter 4: IF THIS EDUCATION FAILS, WHO PUSHES IT?

1. Two paragraphs. Coulson, W. R. 1987. Does therapy belong in the classroom? *Education Reporter* (November): Number 22: page 4.

2. Ibid.

3. Coulson, W. R. 1989. Promoting the disastrous pop psychologies of the '60s: page 1. *The Forum* (August).

4. *Humanist Manifestos One and Two*. 1973. Prometheus Books. NY.

5. Three paragraphs. Ibid.

6. Cox, Harvey. 1965. *The Secular City*. Macmillan. NY.

7. Sentence. Cadman, Charles in introduction of Albert Shanker. 1989. Local.

8. Sentence. Rosche, C. F. 1990. Rep. Boxer PACS it in. *Argus Courier*. Congresswoman gets large sums from special interests (March 2). Petaluma

9. Coulson, W. R. Council on Smoking and Stupidity. 1987. Cigarettes and the self-esteem scam: page 2. *Center for Enterprising Families*. Comptche, CA.

10. Coulson, W. R. 1986. To San Ramon Valley Herald: page 1. Re DECIDE. *USIU*. San Diego.

11. Coulson, W. R. 1987. Chick Koop's breakthrough: page 6. *Social Justice Review* (March, April). La Jolla, CA. Footnote: Bennett and DeLattre. 1978. Moral education in the schools. *The Public Interest, 50:* page 98. (Winter).

12. Coulson, W. R. 1988. On being lobbied. Memo to *Federal Drug Education Curricula Panel* (April 23).

13. Coulson, W. R. Council on Smoking and Stupidity. 1987. Cigarettes and the self-esteem scam: page 2. *Center for Enterprising Families*. Comptche, CA.

14. Coulson, W. R. 1988. On being lobbied: page 6. Memo to *Federal Drug Education Curricula Panel* (April 23).

15. Coulson, W. R. Audio tape on talkshow radio. Host, Boyd.

16. Two paragraphs: Coulson, W. R. 1987. How to talk to kids about homosexuality: page 3. *Research Council on Ethnopsychology*. San Diego.

17. Four + paragraphs. Coulson, W. R. 1988. Focus: Classroom courses promote drugs and sex. *Education Reporter* (June): 3.

18. Coulson, W. R. 1988. To Bayle-Lissick, Sheila. *Coulson, Psychologist* (September 20). San Diego, CA.

19. Coulson, W. R. 1987. How to talk to kids about homosexuality: page 1. *Research Council on Ethnopsychology*. San Diego. Also, 1987. Chick Koop's breakthrough: page 5. *Social Justice Review* (March, April). La Jolla, CA.

20. Coulson, W. R. About 1984. Backlash against the person-centered approach: page 28. For the *German Client-centered Therapy Association*.

21. Coulson, W. R. and Jan Mikelson. Audio tape. Radio talkshow on WHO.

Chapter 5: WHY DOES THIS EDUCATION CAUSE HARM?

1. Coulson, W. R. 1989. To Johnson, Mark L., M..D.: page 3. *Research Council on Ethnopsychology* (June 17). La Jolla, CA.
2. Three paragraphs. Coulson, W. R. 1987. Principled morality vs. consequentialism: page 1. *Research Council on Ethnopsychology*. San Diego.
3. Coulson, W. R. Videotape: Saturday A. M. Southeast Christian Church. Louisville, KY.
4. Coulson, W. R. 1987. Home economics text cited, Does therapy belong in the classroom ? *Education Reporter* (November): Number 22: page 4.
5. Four paragraphs: Coulson and Boyd. Audio tape of radio talkshow.
6. Sentence. Ibid.
7. Seven paragraphs. Coulson, W. R. 1987. Principled morality vs. consequentialism: page 1. *Research Council on Ethnopsychology*. San Diego.
8. Coulson, W. R. 1989. To Johnson, Mark L., M..D. *Research Council on Ethnopsychology* (June 17). La Jolla, CA. Also, about 1984. Backlash against the person-centered approach: page 14. For the *German Client-centered Therapy Association*.
9. Two paragraphs. Coulson, W. R. 1981. Lecture Notes: page 8. *USIU Psychology 640: Life-Cycle Human Development* (Fall). San Diego.
10. Two paragraphs. Coulson, W. R. 1987. Principled morality vs. consequentialism. *Research Council on Ethnopsychology*. San Diego.
11. Four paragraphs. Coulson, W. R. About 1984. Backlash against the person-centered approach: pp. 1, 5, 6, also footnote 2. For the *German Client-centered Therapy Association*.
12. Three paragraphs. Coulson, W. R. 1980. From client-centered therapy to the person-centered approach and back again: page 3. *Panel Discussion at the University of San Diego* (August 2). San Diego.
13. Coulson, W. R. 1983. Tearing down the temple: Confessions of a Catholic school dismantler. *Fidelity* (December): 18 - 22.
14. Two sentences. Coulson, W. R. About 1984. Backlash against the person-centered approach: page 2. For the *German Client-centered Therapy Association*.
15. Sentence. Pereira, Joseph. 1989. Alarming result: Even a school that is leading the drug war grades itself a failure: Students say why Bainbridge, after a 12-year effort, hasn't stemmed abuse. Struggling to interest parents. Wall Street Journal: Vol. CXXI No. 93 (November 10).
16. Sentence. Coulson, W. R. 1983. Tearing down the temple: Confessions of a Catholic school dismantler: page 19.*Fidelity* (December): 18 - 22.
17. "Perfectionism": Coulson, W. R. About 1984. Backlash against the person-centered approach: page 11. For the *German Client-centered Therapy Association*.
18. Two paragraphs. Coulson, W. R. 1981. Lecture Notes: page 7. *USIU Psychology 640: Life-Cycle Human Development* (Fall). San Diego.

19. Sentence. Coulson, W. R. About 1984. Backlash against the person-centered approach: page 2. For the *German Client-centered Therapy Association.*
20. Coulson, W. R. and Carl Rogers.1968.From the manuscript of Second edition of *On Having No Choice:* page 4. Columbus, OH.
21. Ibid.: page 5 (273 in text).
22. Sentence. Coulson, W. R. About 1984. Backlash against the person-centered approach: page 14. For the *German Client-centered Therapy Association.*
23. Sentence. Ibid.: page 14.
24. Sentence. Ibid.: page 17.
25. Mesterton-Gibbons, Karen. 1990. Is smaller better? *Newsweek:* (March 12).
26. Coulson, William R. 1987. Abstinence best Aids defense. *The San Diego Union* (July 23): Commentary B-11.

Chapter 6: WHAT EDUCATION WORKS?

1. Half paragraph. Coulson, W. R. 1983. Lenten Obligations. *Fidelity* (April).
2. Coulson, W. R. 1977. Don't coddle the piano player: page 120. *San Diego Magazine* (June).
3. Coulson, W. R. 1981. Lecture Notes. *USIU Psychology 640: Life-Cycle Human Development:* page 12. (Fall). San Diego.
4. Coulson, W. R. 1989. Videotape: Saturday A. M. Southeast Christian Church. Louisville, KY.
5. Nine paragraphs: William R. Coulson. 1977. Don't coddle the piano player. *San Diego Magazine* (June): 119-122.
6. Four paragraphs. Coulson, W. R. 1986. Killers of culture: page 20. *Fidelity* (March).
7. Coulson, W. R. I'm no masterpiece. *Magnificat. Center for Enterprising Families.* La Jolla, CA.
8. Coulson, W. R. 1977. Don't coddle the piano player: page 120. *San Diego Magazine* (June).
9. Three paragraphs. Coulson, W. R. 1981. Lecture Notes: page 12. *USIU Psychology 640: Life-Cycle Human Development* (Fall). San Diego.
10. Three paragraphs. Coulson, W. R. To Dr. Luoto, Joanne and Dr. David Sundwald, et al: page 5. *Project Mozart* (January 30). La Jolla, CA.
11. Ibid.: pp. 5, 6.
12. Two paragraphs: Shirk, George. 1990. Sarunas gets a decree: "I can't be patient anymore," Nelson says. *San Francisco Chronicle:* (January 8).
13. Thirteen paragraphs. Coulson, W. R. 1978. What to do with a little girl. *Dialogue,* University of Kansas (Winter).
14. Two paragraphs. Coulson, W. R. 1971. Tips for agents abound in family's European experiences: page 2. *Travel Weekly* (February 9). NY.
15. Sentence. Coulson, W. R. 1981. Lecture Notes: page 10. *USIU Psychology 640: Life-Cycle Human Development* (Fall). San Diego.
16. Three paragraphs: Ibid.

17. Seven paragraphs. Coulson Family Jazz Band. *Banding:* pp. 60 - 63. La Jolla, CA.
18. Four paragraphs. Coulson, W. R. 1986. Neversmoke responds to the corrupting of schoolchildren. *Mendocino County Substance Abuse Newsletter* (Summer). Mendocino County, CA.
19. Five paragraphs. Coulson, W. R. 1987. How to talk to kids about homosexuality: pp. 1, 6. *Research Council on Ethnopsychology.* San Diego.

Chapter 7: TIMELESS PRINCIPLES FOR GOOD EDUCATION

1. Coulson, W. R. Video tape: Education that harms good children. Southeast Christian Church. Louisville, KY.
2. Coulson, W. R. Ethnopsychology. 1985. *Talk to the Association of Christian Therapists* (October 15). Estes Park, CO.
3. Three paragraphs. An obscenity in psychology. *Project Mozart.* La Jolla, CA.
4. Sentence. 1979. *The Strength Test:* page 3. La Jolla, CA.
5. Three paragraphs. Coulson, W. R. 1977. The foreignness of feelings. *The La Jolla Experiment: Eight Personal Views.* La Jolla, CA.
6. Coulson, W. R. 1981. Lecture Notes: page 8. *USIU Psychology 640: Life-Cycle Human Development* (Fall). San Diego.
   Also, Polanyi, Michael. 1958. *Personal Knowledge.* Chicago.
7. Two paragraphs. Coulson, W. R. 1977. Don't coddle the piano player: page 122. *San Diego Magazine* (June): 119-122.
8. Coulson, W. R. Video tape: Education that harms. *Southeast Christian Church.* Louisville, KY.
9. Coulson, W. R. About 1984. Backlash against the person-centered approach: page 8. For the *German Client-centered Therapy Association.*
10. Ibid.: page 7
11. Coulson, W. R. 1981. Lecture Notes: page 11. *USIU Psychology 640: Life-Cycle Human Development* (Fall). San Diego.
12. Sentence. Ibid.: page 9.
13. Coulson, W. R. and Jeannie. An invitation to inquire about conviction. *Center for the Recovery of Conviction.* La Jolla, CA.
14. Coulson, W. R. Coulson, W. R. 1981. Lecture Notes: page 7. *USIU Psychology 640: Life-Cycle Human Development* (Fall). San Diego.
15. Three paragraphs. Ibid.
16. Ibid.: page 10.
17. Penzias, Arno. 1989. *Ideas and Information, Managing in a High-Tech World.* W. W. Norton and Company. NY.

BIBLIOGRAPHY

Blum, Richard, et al. 1976. *Drug Education: Results and Recommendations.* Lexington, MA.

Brook, J. S., M. Whiteman, A. S. Gordon, D. W. Brook. 1983. Fathers and sons. *J Genetic Psychology.*

Chandler, Russell. 1988. New Age Epidemic adapted from *Understanding the New Age.* Irving, TX.

Contemporary Ob/Gym. 1988 (November).

Coulson, William R. 1987. Abstinence best Aids defense. *The San Diego Union* (July 23): Commentary B-11. San Diego.

_____. About 1984. Backlash against the person-centered approach. For the *German Client-centered Therapy Association.*

_____. 1987. The Californication of Carl Rogers. *Fidelity* (November): 20 - 29.

_____. 1987. Chick Koop's breakthrough. *Social Justice Review* (March, April). La Jolla, CA.

_____. 1989. Concerning Quest. To Mrs. Terry Fennig. *Research Council on Ethnopsychology* (February 15)). San Diego.

_____. Confessions of an ex-sexologist. 1988. *Social Justice Review* (March/April): 43 - 47.

_____. Coulson Family Jazz Band. *Banding:* 60 - 63. La Jolla, CA.

_____. 1984. Defenseless children. *Project Mozart* (November 21). La Jolla, CA.

_____. 1987. Does therapy belong in the classroom? *Education Reporter* (November): Number 22: 1 - 4.

_____. 1977. Don't coddle the piano player. *San Diego Magazine* (June): 119-122.

_____. 1979. The enterprising family. *The Strength Test:* 8 - 15. La Jolla, CA.

_____. Ethnopsychology. 1985. *Talk to the Association of Christian Therapists* (October 15). Estes Park, CO.

_____. 1985. Ethnopsychology and the principle of polycentricity. *Project Mozart* (July). La Jolla, CA.

_____. Experimenting on children. *Research Council on Ethnopsychology.* San Diego.

_____. 1984. Expert: Parents should push kids. [and a parent's response] *United Press International* (May).

_____. 1988. Focus: Classroom courses promote drugs and sex. *Education Reporter* (June): 3.

_____. 1977. The foreignness of feelings. *The La Jolla Experiment: Eight Personal Views.* La Jolla, CA.

_____. 1989. Founder of "value-free" education says he owes parents an apology. *AFA Journal* (April): 20, 21

_____. 1980. From client-centered therapy to the person-centered approach and back again. Panel Discussion at the University of San Diego (August 2). San Diego.

_____. 1989. From the manuscript of the second edition of *On Having No*

Choice. Research Council on Ethnopsychology. San Diego, CA.

_____. Re Helping Youth Decide. Comptche, CA.

_____. 1985. Re Helping Youth Decide. *Project Mozart* (July 15). La Jolla, CA.

_____. 1985. Re Helping Youth Decide: Fox/geese. *New York State Journal of Medicine:* Vol. 85 (July). NY.

_____. How to prevent another Mozart. *Project Mozart*. Comptche, CA.

_____. 1987. How to talk to kids about homosexuality. *Research Council on Ethnopsychology*. San Diego.

_____. 1982. Hugging your kid and beyond. *Clinical and Counseling Psychology* (May). La Jolla and Comptche, CA.

_____. I'm no masterpiece. *Magnificat*. Center for Enterprising Families. La Jolla, CA.

_____. An invitation from Bill & Jeannie Coulson to inquire about conviction. *Center for the Recovery of Conviction*. La Jolla, CA.

_____. 1986. Killers of culture. *Fidelity* (March): 19 - 27.

_____. 1981. Lecture Notes. *USIU Psychology 640: Life-Cycle Human Development* (Fall). San Diego.

_____. 1983. Lenten Obligations. *Fidelity* (April).

_____. 1978. Life is a jazz band. *Dialogue: A Kansas Journal of Health Concerns* (Winter). University of Kansas.

_____. 1986. Neversmoke responds to the corrupting of schoolchildren. *Mendocino County Substance Abuse Newsletter* (Summer). Mendocino County, CA.

_____. 1988. On being lobbied. Memo to *Federal Drug Education Curricula Panel* (April 23).

_____. An obscenity in psychology. *Project Mozart*. La Jolla, CA.

_____. 1986. On the value—indeed, the inevitability—of absolutes. *Parents' Health Initiative* (March). Comptche, CA.

_____. 1987. Principled morality vs. consequentialism. *Research Council on Ethnopsychology*. San Diego.

_____. 1989. Promoting the disastrous pop psychologies of the '60s. *The Forum* (August).

_____. 1984. Proverbs called valuable tool in dealing with life. *AP Newsfeatures* (June 29). San Diego.

_____. 1988. Questianity and the politics of behavioral science. *School of Human Behavior, United States International University* (May 10). San Diego.

_____. 1987. Reclaiming client-centered counseling from the person-centered movement. *Center for Enterprising 'Families*. Comptche, CA.

_____. 1989. The Seventh Sense: Case studies of parents protecting their children. *Center for Enterprising Families*. La Jolla, CA.

_____. 1989. Sex Education Research. To concerned parent. *Director, Graduate Program in General Psychology, United States International University* (February 6). San Diego.

_____. 1979. *The Strength Test*. Helicon House. La Jolla, CA.

_____. Tapes: two video and two audio.

_____. 1983. Tearing down the temple: Confessions of a Catholic school dismantler.*Fidelity* (December): 18 - 22.

_____. 1972. Tips for agents abound in family's European experiences. *Travel Weekly* (April 14). NY.

_____. 1988. To Bayle-Lissick, Sheila. *Coulson, Psychologist* (September 20). San Diego, CA.

_____. 1986. To Editor, San Ramon Valley Herald, Danville, CA. Professor at *United States International University*. San Diego.

_____. 1989. To Johnson, Mark L., M..D. *Research Council on Ethnopsychology* (June 17). San Diego.

_____. 1985. To Dr. Luoto, Joanne and Dr. David Sundwald, et al. *Project Mozart* (January 30). La Jolla, CA.

_____. 1986. To Mount Diablo Area Parents Concerned with DECIDE. *Neversmoke* (June 5). Mendocino County, CA.

_____. 1984. To push away the malevolent stranger. *Ethnopsychology Institute*. Comptche, CA.

_____. 1986. To San Ramon Valley Herald. Re DECIDE. *USIU*. San Diego.

_____. 1988. To Wolpert, John. *United States International University* (May 12). San Diego.

_____. 1978. What to do with a little girl. *Dialogue*. University of Kansas (Winter).

_____. 1971. Why do people travel? *Travel Weekly* (February 9). NY.

Coulson, W. R. and Carl Rogers.1968. Second edition of *On Having No Choice*. Columbus, OH.

Council on Smoking and Stupidity. 1987. Cigarettes and the self-esteem scam. *Center for Enterprising Families*. Comptche, CA.

Cox, Harvey. 1965. *The Secular City*. Macmillan. NY.

Doctoral candidate, international student. Drug education (in his son's public school). *United States International University (USIU)*. San Diego.

Evans, Richard. 1981. *Dialogue with Carl Rogers*. NY.

Gordon, Thomas. 1974. *T.E.T. Teacher Effectiveness Training*. NY.

Hanson, Dan. 1986. Humanism bias found in textbooks? *Eastern Shore Courier* (October 19). Fairhope, AL.

Hoffman, Edward. 1988. *The Right to Be Human*. Jeremy Tarcher. Los Angeles.

Kirschenbaum, Howard. 1979. *On Becoming Carl Rogers*. Delacorte Press. NY.

Kurz, Paul, ed. 1973*Humanist Manifestos One and Two*. Buffalo, NY

Maslow, Abraham. 1979. Humanistic Education vs. Professional Education: Further Reflections. *Journal of Humanistic Psychology*. (Summer).

_____. 1970. Humanistic Education vs. Professional Education. *New Directions in Teaching* 2: 3 - 10.

_____. 1979. *The Journals of A. H. Maslow. Vols. 1 and 2*. Brooks/Cole. Monterey, CA.

_____. 1970. *Motivation and Personality*. Rev. Ed. NY.

_____. 1965. The taboo of tenderness. A lecture at Brandeis University.

McCormack, Patricia. 1984. Parents need to pass along their talents. *Daily News*

(June 10). NY.

Mesterton-Gibbons, Karen. 1990. Is smaller better? *Newsweek* (March 12).

National Association of State Boards of Education. 1986. *Helping Youth Decide.*

National Association of State Boards of Education. 1987. *Helping Youth Say No.*

Parma, Drew. 1988. Drug, sex education plan criticized. *Tribune-Herald.* (August 30): B. Waco, TX.

Penzias, Arno. 1989. *Ideas and Information, Managing in a High-Tech World.* W. W. Norton and Company. NY.

Pereira, Joseph. 1989. Alarming result: Even a school that is leading the drug war grades itself a failure: Students say why Bainbridge, after a 12-year effort, hasn't stemmed abuse. Struggling to interest parents. Wall Street Journal: Vol. CXXI No. 93: (November 10).

Polanyi, Michael. 1969. Marjorie Grene, editor. The message of the Hungarian Revolution. *Knowing and Being.* Chicago.

_____. 1958. *Personal Knowledge.* Chicago.

Polanyi & Prosch. 1975. Page 203.

Read, Donald, Sidney Simon, Joel Goodman. 1977. *Health Education: The Search for Values:* Page 152. Engelwood.

Rogers, Carl. 1980. *A Way of Being.* Boston.

_____. 1972. *Becoming Partners: Marriage and Its Alternatives.* NY.

_____. 1980. Carl. 1969. *Freedom to Learn.* Columbus, OH.

_____. 1983. *Freedom to Learn for the 80's.* Columbus, OH.

Rosche, C. F. 1990. Rep. Boxer PACS it in. *Argus Courier* (March 2). Petaluma.

Shirk, George. 1990. Sarunas gets a decree: "I can't be patient anymore," Nelson says. *San Francisco Chronicle* (January 8).

Slavicek, Anne. 1988. Give the gift of independence. *San Diego Press* (September): 21

Thwaites, Lynette. 1985. Project Mozart teaches old-fashioned values. *La Jolla Light* (July 11). Las Jolla, CA.

Wilson, D., G. Wood, N. Johnston, J. Sicurella. 1982. Randomized clinical trial supportive follow-up for cigarette smokers in a family practice. *Can Med Asso J* 126:1270129.

Yankelovich, Skelly, and White, Inc. 1976. A study of cigarette smoking among teenage girls and young women. Unpublished report for The American Cancer Society: Feb. And 1977. Summary published: Publication No. [NIH] 77-1203.

Small Helm Press interprets direction in contemporary life.

Forthcoming book by Pearl Evans: *WHAT'S A KID TO BELIEVE?*
For kids at school coping with controversial concepts. Practical, easy
reading for middle and high school kids. Of interest to parents, too.

Three Small Helm books—first two paperbacks and third one hardcover:

FAITH'S CHECKBOOK by Charles H. Spurgeon, 224 pages. Guidance.
New Topical Edition in modern English. Classical devotional.
365 scriptural promises and comments indexed to match your needs

CHINA: THE LION AND THE DRAGON by Pearl Evans, 304 pages.
A personal interpretation of Chinese life, customs, background. Evans
lived and taught as the only foreigner in her college community in
1984/1985. Illustrated.

MARX OR JESUS:Two Men—Two Plans by Pearl Evans. 160 pages.
Hardcover. Fascinating study contrasting the principles, lives, influence,
manifestos (texts included), and targeted enemies of these two leaders.

- - - - cut here or write note -

ORDER FORM   *Small Helm Press*   707-763-5757
                     622-A Baker Street
                     Petaluma, CA 94952

Please send me the following marked items:

_____ copies, HIDDEN DANGER IN THE CLASSROOM
_____ copies, FAITH'S CHECKBOOK   @$12.95
_____ copies, CHINA: The Lion and the Dragon   @$14.95
_____ copies, MARX OR JESUS: Two Men—Two Plans   @$17.95
_____ Please send information about WHAT'S A KID TO BELIEVE?
_____ After reading HIDDEN DANGER, I enclose comments.

In California only, add 6% tax.
Shipping: Paperback, $2.00 first copy; hardcover, $2.50, first copy.
TOTAL ENCLOSED $_____
I understand I may return any book for full refund if not satisfied.

NAME AND ADDRESS WITH ZIP:

_____

_____

_____